Endorsements

"Bobby Howard's book, *The Father's Heart,* takes on some of the complex issues that have held generations of Christians from moving into their promised freedom. This book is bold and will prove challenging to much of the religious tradition of today, but the work is greatly needed and graciously presented.

> *'If we give people a better, more faithful lover, they will eventually leave their sin behind.'*

This book could be the gift you've been looking for in your personal journey to the Father's heart."
—Steve Dixon
Lead Pastor, Christian Life Cathedral
Fayetteville, Arkansas

"Every generation has taken some issue with its predecessors, and rightly so, as the imperfection of people and the Church demand that our institutions be constantly awakened and realigned to God's original design. However, few 'critics' identify the real fundamental issues, and even fewer give substantial solutions. Bobby Howard has not only put his finger on the right issues of our 'religiosity,' but also gracefully pointed us in the right direction toward our liberty and acceptance in Christ. This 'kid' has done us all a big favor by writing this book! Read it!"
—Alan Platt
Founder and Leader of Doxa Deo Ministries & the City Changers
Movement
Pretoria, South Africa

"I believe that Bobby Howard's book, *The Father's Heart*, carries the message and the cure for an emotionally depleted and fatherless generation. This book may very well be a classic work written prophetically over a generation, and it may stand as the banner message that leads them into 'another Exodus.' Drink deeply."
—*Josh Foliart*
Founder of MULTIPLi
Lima, Peru

"Pastors like me need to read books like Bobby Howard's to gain insight into young adults whose stories are similar to his and to remind us that we need to practice what we preach. That is, if we believe the Gospel proclamation that the God of Jesus Christ is a God of love, then we should trust that love to work its transforming power through our ministries and not try to do the Holy Spirit's job of conviction. Thank you, Bobby, for sharing."
—*Rev. Rodney Steele*
Senior Pastor, First United Methodist Church
Mountain Home, Arkansas

The Father's Heart

Another Exodus

Bobby Howard

The Father's Heart
Bobby Howard

Well Water Publishing
Fayetteville, AR

Library of Congress Control Number: 2013918566

Printed in the United States of America

ISBN: 978-1-940243-14-6

I dedicate this work to those who breathed life into it: Mom and Dad, Pastor Josh Foliart, Pastor Monte Henderson, Pastor Steve Dixon, Mr. Gary McGlaughlin, Lexy, Kyle, Morgan, Chad, Niki, Tim, Zac, Jessica, and many others. This project floats only because of your encouragement and blessing.

Acknowledgments

I would like to thank my mom and dad for being great parents. They released me into God's will, right when they needed to release me. Mom and Dad have spent the last twenty-two years of their lives serving me, and I am so grateful for them. Their love and patience have made this possible.

I would like to thank Pastor Josh Foliart for teaching me, and many others, how to dream big dreams. Pastor Josh has been a blessing throughout the writing process, and he told me simply to "go for it" multiple times. I finally listened. He, his wife, Casandra, and his two children serve as models in my life of a ministry-driven, godly family.

I would like to thank my friends who have supported this crazy project. God has blessed my life with some incredible people. They continue to believe and pray the impossible with me.

Table of Contents

Foreword

The book in your hand could be the cure for a disease that is more dangerous than cancer: religion. It was written by a young man with a sincere and competent desire for his own generation to see what he has seen and hear what he has heard. I believe that the message in this book is one that must resound through every sermon and through every piece of Kingdom art and media, no matter the title or topic. *The Father's Heart* is the message behind the message, and we can't afford to miss it.

The youngest generation walking the earth today is a generation searching for a father. Whether referring to those who have no father to speak of or those left unfathered by an emotionally absent male figure—fatherlessness is endemic in our day. Hardly any today have not had their lives negatively affected by fatherlessness in some form or fashion.

Just as with any disease, fatherlessness has symptoms. The primary symptom of this fatherless generation is the misjudgment of the character of our Father in heaven.

Not too long ago, I was speaking with a Christian leader. Our conversation centered on our commonly understood need for the Gospel's great and forceful advancement into the eastern parts of the earth (sometimes referred to as the "10/40 Window"). However, when I called his attention to the great need we have for the Gospel in the western parts of the world, he asked me to explain my thoughts. I spoke with him about the generation that was born after 1990 and the advent of the Internet, explaining that this young demographic represents at least one third of the world's population. I said, "I'm afraid the reason that many of these young hearts are not engaging Christianity is because our message has left them without a clear picture of the good character of the Father."

Just as the young businessman of Matthew 25:24-25 misjudged the character of the master and hence buried his talent in the ground, so the members of this unique and potentially powerful generation are burying their heads in the fear of religion. They have seen it at its worst, and they want nothing to do with its dogmatic and scandalous ways.

However, if you talk with them about the God of the Bible, and about His heart toward injustice and ensuring freedom for captive daughters, you will get quite a different response from them. If you speak to them of His desire not to judge, but to justify those who have wounded Him deeply, you can capture the attention of this often misguided, young demographic, and they will see the heroic mercy and justice of God in a new light. If you retell the stories and doctrines of the Old and New Testaments in light of the God's heart and His desire for all of humankind to share in His inheritance, this generation's ears perk up, and their attention spans linger miraculously.

This generation must grasp what the author says so well:

"What if Jesus's sacrifice was never meant to be the measure of our shame? What if His death, instead, was the measure of God's love for us? What if Jesus's blood was never meant to highlight our depravity, but instead meant to show the inner workings (literally!) of God's heart? What if the slain Lamb isn't a statement of our weakness and sin, but God's statement of our worth to Him? What if Jesus's death was the Bridegroom's ultimate pursuit of His Bride, the perfect invitation into a true love story? What if the cross was a value statement? What if it were no longer an instrument of shame?"

Amen.

The message of the cross is not about us, just as the Christian life is not about us. It's about Christ. It's about His desire. We are simply the object of that immense and unyielding desire.

In my opinion, the above quote acts as the hinge of the rest of the message you are about to read (or, more accurately, drink). I believe that Bobby Howard's book, *The Father's Heart*, carries the message and the cure for an emotionally depleted and fatherless generation. This book very well may be a classic work, written prophetically over a generation, standing as the banner message that leads them into "another exodus." Drink deeply.

Josh Foliart

Founder of MULTIPLi

Lima, Peru

JoshFoliart.com

Introduction

I am just one of very many young adult believers who represent the future of the Church. My generation is faced with some dangerous hurdles: we don't know who God is, we don't know who we are, and we don't know the Father's heart toward us.

What factors gave rise to these problems? The Christian faith presented to much of this generation was called "Good News," while at the same time, many people were called "sinners," "depraved," or "unworthy" of God's love (which is hardly good news). Many were taught that Jesus loves them, while at the same time, conditioned to walk in a false humility and identity that can only be motivated by shame. So many were promised a faith that would give them life, but instead received a religious knowledge that would ultimately lead them to self-rejection, shame, or condemnation. You can call it Good News all you want, but if the news doesn't sound good or make sense to the hearer, it probably is *not* Good News.

Let down or disappointed by what was presented as good and branded as the Gospel, a huge portion of my generation has turned away in search of something else—something that works better. Many young people have taken the exit ramp off the traditional and denominational forms of Christianity. Many, unfortunately, have dropped their Christian faith altogether.

That is why I have written this book. Too many of my fellow young people need healing and freedom. Too many need God-breathed identity and purpose. Burned, far too many have simply walked away from Jesus.

It is my generation's assigned task to reclaim our faith. Everything we build on the earth will be built on the foundation of what we discover to be true, so it's important that we discover rightly. It is our task to reclaim for our own generation the timeless truths of God's Kingdom and leave behind the religious baggage we have carried (which is neither easy nor light).

We need to revisit the cross. The story of the cross needs to be retold so that it can shine as brightly for the world today as it did the day Christ was nailed to it. The cross and the grace of Christ are scandalous. They do not fit into "religion" or our weak attempts to systematize a relationship with God. Yet we continue to choose religion; therefore, we continue to choose bondage.

I have subtitled this book *Another Exodus* because when I see my generation of fellow believers, I see multitudes enslaved in Egypt or wandering the desert, all the while professing faith in God (just like Israel in the book of Exodus). Jesus said that where His Spirit is, there would be liberty, yet so many believers in our day are not *free*. This is a problem. We have embraced Christian belief, but something about our faith is not working right. The boldness, joy, and liberty of Christ do not yet mark us. I see in us another Israel in bondage, in need of deliverance. Thus, we need another exodus.

In this book, I share what I have learned about the Father's heart. These truths have begun to set me free, and it is my prayer that they will begin to set others free as well. The cross, prodigal love, desert seasons, Eden, weakness, and our identity in Christ— I've addressed these topics in the hope that a new light will be cast onto our generation's relationship with the Father. Many do not know who the Father is, and I hope these words help to reveal Him.

I present this work to you in humility, understanding that I have not presented all the answers. Read my words prayerfully, testing everything, and ask the Father to breathe life into your faith. I hope you enjoy *The Father's Heart.* I pray that this message finds a home somewhere in your heart.

Part 1

Crosses and Deserts

CHAPTER 1

FOR GOD SO LOVED THE WORLD

I still remember the moment I was saved. I was sitting in a boring room in the youth wing at church, and I did not want to be there. I could have been watching cartoons, or sleeping, or playing Poké-mon. Really, if I'd had the choice, I would have been just about any-where other than in that room.

It was confirmation class, and our teacher was an uninspir-ing, traditional clergyman who felt compelled to speak over our heads in flowery, doctrinal language. The man used handfuls of ten-dollar words that I probably still cannot define, and he really didn't connect with us young people (or we didn't connect with him—whichever).

I did not like church. I did not enjoy sitting and listening to peo-ple tell me how much I needed to change. As a kid, it wasn't as if my life was difficult or broken, so why were all these people talking about me being a broken sinner?

"Sinner." That's a great way to get kids to enjoy church—call them evil.

Tell them about Hell, fire, and wrath. "God hates..." These are only half-truths. A Father of fire or pain is not a Father young children want to approach. Nor is it the Father described in the Gospel.

I am not bitter (honestly). However, my experience is one shared in common with many thousands of people today, and an experience that falls short.

At that time in my life, I was still halfway expecting my letter from Hogwarts to arrive, hopeful that the owl was only lost or something. I wanted to go fight Lord Voldemort with Harry Potter. Professor Dumbledore was probably my favorite person alive, and he was just a character in a book. So it is understandable that an uninspiring, gray cinderblock church building wasn't very enticing to me.

At that point in my life, I was thirsty for something magical. I was thirsty for a fantastic world in which things work out for the good guys, all the time. I was thirsty for a reality in which the boring, natural, and unredeemed life I was experiencing was only the surface of what was really happening. So young, I had a thirst for a more fascinating world. I just knew, deep down, that there was more. (I have since discovered that I was right.)

As children, we have access to gifts from God that, regardless of belief, call us to open our eyes and see past mundane, everyday life. More so when we are younger, I think, He calls out to us in our imaginations and our dreams, telling us, "There is more, keep looking, for there is more."

I believe we experience God when we are young. We just don't know who He is. We hear His voice and we see things happen, but we don't know who is talking. Then, as we get older, we are told that magic doesn't happen. So we quit looking for it. We shut our eyes and stop up our ears with unbelief, denying the mysterious a place in our lives. We harden to something bigger than ourselves, to something we cannot necessarily explain. We harden to something exciting and supernatural.

Something like God.

As a kid, thirsty for something more, I entertained myself with fiction and stories about magical worlds like Harry Potter's. I read all the books that were banned from the Bible Belt's public school libraries. I played role-playing games. I watched cartoons and traded Pokémon cards. I wanted to be the very best, the best there ever was (Pokémon joke). I did whatever it took to keep my mind fascinated with fantastic things—whatever.

Somewhere along the way, though, I failed to realize the truth that the actual creator of the universe is far more magical and fascinating than any of the worldly creations and imaginations I enjoyed. I did not know it, but some of the fiction I read actually fell pretty close to the mark of truth, as far as supernatural things go. Battles between good and evil are real. There are real heroes, and "destiny" isn't just a word that makes us feel good. I did not know it, but God is truly fantastic. (I had thought He was boring, and that He did not like me.) I was fascinated with wands and Yu-Gi-Oh! battles and all the other stuff that I had pumped into my imagination, but did not know that God is infinitely better than all of it. If only I had understood the reality that God makes fiction look boring, I would have loved church.

Anyway, back to my salvation: dry class, boring teacher, dry and boring God. My salvation was very ordinary. When we came to the end of the confirmation course, our pastor expected us to place our faith in Christ. He asked each of us if we believed Jesus is Lord, and everyone said, "Yes." I confessed with my mouth that Jesus was Lord, and I think I probably believed it a little, too. At least, I knew I was supposed to believe it. I don't know how much of my heart was in it, but in that moment, God met me right where I was. I did not believe what I had verbally confessed with my whole heart, but my weak faith added to God's willingness to meet me was enough. God began to reel me in.

****

Grace. In that moment, my life didn't drastically change, but my eternity did.

That I am sitting in a coffee shop writing this book about God's love is a testament to the fact that God answered my half-hearted faith in that boring little room. I did not love God with my whole heart in that moment, but when I called Him my Lord, He began a process in me that has come to save both my soul and my life. About a decade later— today—I know and experience His love for me.

(Though I am still waiting on my letter from Hogwarts.)

SOMETHING WRONG

Many Christians in my generation have been told many confusing lies. It's a systemic problem that we need to confront. We have an inaccurate picture of God. We don't know who the Father is. If we do know who the Father is, we often misunderstand His heart. We think our faith has a lot more to do with us than it actually does. We look at the cross and see our sin. We look at the slain Jesus and see our shame. We see things through our own fallen eyes and lenses rather than from God's vantage point.

We sometimes fail to understand that the protagonist of our faith is the Father's heart toward us, and not ourselves or the sin that would come between God and us. However, we can step out of our wrong beliefs. We must. We can reclaim our faith. We can rebuild it upon the foundation of the heart of the Father.

If we do not fix our perspective, our generation will continue to walk in the bondage, pain, and shame that we are so accustomed to, and we will pass on this same shame to the generations that follow us—sin, chains, our broken pasts, and all. They will stick around until a revelation of the heart of the Father removes them from us. We cannot be a generation marked by freedom if we continue to enslave ourselves to something less than absolute liberty (hence, *Another Exodus*).

What if we revisit the cross? What if we let go of all the baggage we typically carry around with it? What if we boil down the foundation of our faith—the cross—to what it was supposed to mean to us?

The cross itself—Jesus's mission—is not our problem. The cross is God's perfect plan. God's perfect plan has never been the problem. The problem is what Christians have made the cross into and how we have misunderstood God's heart. As a result, we profess our faith in Christ, yet we walk enslaved lives. We buy into "truth," yet we walk through life governed by lies. We worship the Spirit of liberty with our mouths, yet we bow our hearts to the much cheaper powers of bondage in this world.

Something is out of whack. The bland reality we experience and the grand reality promised by the things we claim to believe are two very different things. What we *actually* experience as a product of what we *actually* believe falls far short of the promises in Scripture that declare freedom, light, and truth in the life of the believer in Christ. So many put their faith in Christ, yet too many of that same number walk enslaved, back in Egypt.

Hopefully you can see the vast disconnect. Slavery in Egypt: addiction, depression, anxiety, torn families, moral falls, broken relationships, condemnation, self-loathing, and more. Something is wrong with what we believe if our faith in Jesus Christ is not setting us free from the devastating fallout of sin. Sin will be in the earth until the Father makes things new, but we can be free of its spiritual consequences, power, and bondage right now.

Jesus says we are free in Him, but many of us simply do not live free lives. Supernatural freedom, joy, and peace should be commonplace for the believer in Christ. But where I live, among believers in my generation, they are not commonplace.

It is a straightforward issue: something is wrong. Sin and its consequences have a prevalent place in our theology, and their power has a prevalent place in our lives. This is not OK. It's time we reevaluate how and what we believe.

THE ROOT

Freedom starts at the foundation of everything we believe: the cross.

Think hard on the implications of these questions: What if Jesus's sacrifice was never meant to be the measure of our shame? What if His death, instead, was the measure of God's love for us? What if Jesus's blood was never meant to highlight our depravity, but instead meant to show the inner workings (literally!) of God's heart? What if the slain Lamb isn't a statement of our weakness and sin, but God's statement of our worth to Him? What if Jesus's death was the Bridegroom's ultimate pursuit of His Bride, the perfect invitation into a true love story? What if the cross was a value statement? What if it were no longer an instrument of shame?

That's a lot of questions. What I'm getting at is this: As Christians, we desperately need to get over our sin identity, which was crucified with Christ. We need an understanding of the Gospel built on the love of God, and not on the total depravity of man. This calls for a fundamental paradigm shift, a change in perspective.

Our relationship with God, which happened only because of the cross, should be much less about our sin and much more about our Father's love. We have built our theology on man's condition and not on God's heart, failing to realize that a "Christian" theology built on sin is just one more man-made religion bound to lure its adherents into painful bondage. If we establish our fallen state as the center of the universe, as the one thing that motivates all of God's interactions with man, we have totally missed the point of

God's love. Therein lies the root of our problem: *some have totally missed the point of God's love.*

We have bought into a religious system built on sin and are locked into slavery because of it. We need a theology built on the heart of the Father and not on the condition of man. Our freedom needs a holy foundation.

> *But God demonstrates his own love for us in this: While we were still sinners, Christ died for us. (Romans 5:8)*

When we allow our sin to motivate our relationship with God rather than God's love, our sin mediates our faith. Because of this, multitudes must first pass through their sin to get to God's love. With sin at the center of our relationship with God, we behold our sin rather than beholding Christ and His work in us. We do everything in our faith through the filter of sin rather than through the filter of Christ, and then wonder why we lack joy, power, and freedom. We are a sin-centered generation, and we must uproot ourselves in order to become centered in God's heart for us.

Our sin focus is a bondage that allows no freedom. It places a very low ceiling on our walk with God.

There is no freedom, trying to walk in the realities of "sin" and "God" at the same time. The realities of "depravity" and "in Christ" cannot be reconciled. An individual can only identify with one because both are jealous and exclusive lovers.

We can confront this confusion. After the cross, are we condemned or are we seated with Christ? Are we dirty or are we made perfect? Are we free from our sin identity or are we not free? We get to choose our reference point, and we cannot have both.

For the believer in Christ, claiming the right identity will make all the difference in the world. It changes how we approach the

Father. It changes what we expect in faith from Christ, and it changes the kind of fruit we will bear.

****

It never made much sense to me that we talked about our sin and our salvation in the same breath. Yes, I understood that we were saved from our sin. However, if we really were "saved" from our sin—past tense—why did we still talk about it so much? Couldn't we move on to a more fantastic subject—something a little more in line with the heart of the Father? His pillars of fire perhaps, or the whirlwind of His glory? The countless histories of God's love and faithfulness which modern storytellers couldn't possibly hope to equal? Warrior angels? Humankind walking the streets of the New Jerusalem? The apostles walking in power? There really are many alternatives to the story of sin.

Sin was never a facet of the heart of our Father, but we talked about it so much in our religious gatherings. Our sin never brought glory to the Father, but we often camped out on the subject.

God is fascinating, but so many in my generation miss this. We miss it because we were told to behold our sin even as we beheld Christ. It's like the two—Christ and sin—held hands. But Christ would never join hands with any lover but you and I. He is faithful.

Our sin has definitely been overemphasized. As a result, an individual's sin—for believer and nonbeliever alike—is too often his or her only point of reference to the Father. Nonbelievers stay distant from the Father because they falsely believe that God's purpose for them includes the identity "sinner." Believers stay distant from the Father because they falsely believe that their identity is still "sinner."

We revolve around our sins, and we only take Jesus along for the ride. Evil has won a great victory by becoming so central to our relationship with our Father.

We are a people who must relearn how to rejoice in the Father, completely removed from our shame. We are burdened to reclaim the type of faith and worship that are absent of our dependence upon "sin." It has become a crutch in the Church's relationship with the Father, and it is only there because it is easy to keep there. We focus on it too much, we reference it too much, and we rely on it too much.

When we lack the faith to embrace new mysteries and the unknown, and when we lack the courage to tread the deepest waters of the Father's heart, we tend to revert back to what we know so well: The story of sin and the root of our personal shame—our present, loud, and familiar reality. Many stay rooted in this spot indefinitely, either paralyzed in their faith or simply comfortable.

****

The cross was not a punishment; it was God's ultimate display of His love for us. Sin, guilt, and shame are not supposed to be tools the Church uses to point people toward Christ. Jesus spent His blood to purchase us from sin, guilt, and shame, which are instruments of the religiously spirited and Satan. God did not nail Jesus to a tree because we are sinners; God nailed Jesus to a tree because He *loves* humanity and is *for* us.

JOHN 3:16

For God so loved the world that he gave his one and only Son, that whoever believes in him shall not perish but have eternal life. (John 3:16)

"For God so loved the world..." Coming from a church background, it is hard to believe that the grand, redemptive plan of God really is as simple as John 3:16. Inoculated with church, it is hard to believe that the entire universe hinges on so few words.

In our attempts to understand why God pursues us and Jesus died for us, we have unnecessarily complicated things. The truth that God gave His Son for us simply because He loves us is absolutely mind-blowing! (As it should be!) It is so simple, yet it changes how we believe. Our redemption required a purchase, but Christ's death was never to be understood as the inevitable conclusion of what would happen when our depravity met God's purity. All along, Christ's death on the cross was to be seen as a fantastic offering of God's love.

John 3:16 doesn't say, "For God so saw our sin..." or "For God so needed an outlet for His wrath..." or "For God was so enraged by our disobedience..." or "For God so felt obligated to answer our sin..." or anything else. None of these things that have worked their way into our personal doctrines or philosophies were motivating factors for the death of Christ at the time John wrote this verse of Scripture.

The Father did not sacrifice His Son for us, bound hopelessly to the one, most painful way by which He could satisfy all of His divine attributes. The Father was not obligated by His character to waste His only begotten Son on behalf of a despicable, depraved, and worthless world. If we take God at His Word in John 3:16, we see the beautiful truth that God gave us Jesus simply because He loves us, even unto death on a cross.

It is so simple. Even childlike.

Somehow, the Father crafted this strategy of the cross from before the foundations of the world as His method for purchasing our souls and winning our hearts. Only Christ's blood could cleanse us, and only such a gift could provoke awe and worship in us. It was perfect: atonement and engagement, tied together in one horrifying, beautiful moment.

Sin as a motivating factor for our faith can only lead to further bondage. All sin can do is enslave and damage. With our sin motivating our relationship with God, we fall in and out of imaginary cycles of righteousness. We work to make ourselves holy and we inevitably let ourselves down. It's slavery. There is no freedom in it. Only God's love motivates freedom.

Christ did not walk into Gethsemane begrudgingly, coerced into death by our sin or by some sense of duty. Indeed, He walked into the garden with blood and anxiety dripping from His pores. He was compelled to that place by love—His own and the Father's love for us. No amount of falling short on our part could ever have twisted Jesus's arm into crucifixion.

The joy set before Jesus in the garden—His motivation—was a restored and mutually loving relationship with His made-perfect Bride.

We have given sin far more power and significance than it is due, and we have made it the center and the engine of the cross, the very climax of all human history. This is backwards. The center and the engine of the cross is the love that God the Father has for His world (John 3:16). Only the incredible love of the Father could possibly have scripted the death of His almighty Son.

WRATH

You might be wondering where God's wrath fits into all this love talk. Wrath was poured out at the cross, but God did it in a way that magnified His love for us. God could have poured out His wrath and brought justice to us in an infinite number of glorious and creative ways, but He chose to do it in a way that proclaimed both His love for us and our worth to Him. He could have revealed Himself as a cold judge, but instead, the Father revealed Himself as having a heart wrecked by passion for Jesus's Bride. That He poured out His wrath on Jesus, in our place and for our salvation, demands that we see His love.

The cross, while an instrument of wrath, is a banner of God's love for us. Never was the Father's wrath expressed, absent of His love.

God did express great disgust at the cross, but His disgust and His wrath were aimed at sin, not at the people whom He had lovingly made in His image. (Jesus became our sin on the cross. His Father actually turned His head away from this tragic sight.)

Put simply: If God's wrath were aimed at us, it would have landed on us. His wrath and justice were poured out to free His children from the sin that would stain them, not to declare His children guilty and wicked. At the cross, we can see clearly that God's holy anger was purposed toward eliminating the things of Satan that would distance God's children from Him.

He is *jealous* for us (Exodus 34:14). He loves us *fiercely*. His wrath and His justice are *for* us, not *against* us. He sees us enslaved to sin and evil (the things that would keep us from Him), and He comes against them in fierce love for us, so that He alone may have our affection. God's agenda at the cross was to provoke us into an eternal and perfect love story. Sin was at the cross, but it was pierced and defeated forever. Wrath was at the cross, but it fell on sin, flowing from the Bridegroom's passion for His Bride.

> *The Lord is compassionate and gracious, slow to anger, abounding in love. He will not always accuse, nor will He harbor His anger forever; He does not treat us as our sins deserve or repay us according to our iniquities. For as high as the heavens are above the earth, so great is His love for those who fear Him; as far as the east is from the west, so far has He removed our transgressions from us. As a father has compassion on his children, so the Lord has compassion on those who fear Him; for He knows how we are formed, He remembers that we are dust. (Psalm 103:8-14)*

A BIT ON HELL

Our generation tends to take issue with Hell. We take issue with a God who calls Himself love and yet simultaneously maintains an eternal Hell. As freethinkers, some of us have taken it upon ourselves to determine that God's wrath, vengeance, and hatred simply cannot be compatible with His love, mercy, and goodness. So we drop one or the other and determine what God can or cannot be like.

That is not what I am doing in this book. Sin is real. Hell is real. Eternity in a lake of fire will be just as real as the cross was. That justice and that pain are very real.

This book is not meant to be a feel good or self-centered message (though God's love *should* provoke bliss, and His affections *are* directed toward those who are centered in Christ). My intention with this book is to share the truth that God loves us. He loved us before we sinned, and our sin failed to change that love. All of God's interactions with creation since the Fall of Humankind have been motivated by His love for us, and they have been aimed at our redemption. His wrath, which is inseparable from the rest of His character, is just another part of the equation of God's love.

We have to get over Hell. It is a needless stumbling block for so many. Yes, Hell is eternal pain, punishment, agony, and more. Yes, in our sin, we justly deserve Hell and wrath. Yes, on the surface, Hell seems unethical and is hard to swallow. But what if Hell—just like the Cross—exists as a result of God's love for His creation? What if the wrath of God pointed at sin and all it consumes is a necessary mirror image of the love of God pointed at Christ's blood and all it consumes? What if Hell is simply another way God loves His children?

That idea seems counterintuitive, but give it a chance. No good father allows his innocent children to be stained by the touch of evil. No good father sees his children fall and does absolutely nothing about it. A good father doesn't settle for distance from the ones he loves.

The "wrath" of the Father is His answer to those things. The cross and Hell—our two big tangible pictures of God's wrath—are God's answers to the fall of the creation that He loves. He pours out His wrath against sin, for the good of all that He loves. His wrath falls on sin and things consumed by sin, for the good of all that is covered by Christ's blood.

What is Hell, if not God's way of eternally separating His children from the influences of evil and those who have chosen evil? It is a fence, separating sheep from goats.

From birth, we are born into Adam's sin and are objects of God's wrath. From new birth in Christ, we are born into Christ's righteousness and are objects of God's affection. Hell is real, but it flows from God's love for His creation. If hellfire and brimstone are real, they most certainly must flow alongside living water. They can only be properly understood in light of God's love. The Bridegroom and the Father are fiercely jealous for the Bride, thus, their wrath against the things that have made her dirty.

> *Strengthen the feeble hands, steady the knees that give*
> *way; say to those with fearful hearts, 'Be strong, do not*
> *fear; your God will come, he will come with vengeance; with*
> *divine retribution he will come to save you.' (Isaiah 35:3-4)*

****

From the moment my soul was saved in that Sunday school class, until about four years ago, I lived in bondage. I did not walk in freedom. I had accepted Christ as my Lord and thought I had a pretty good handle on what God looked like, but my faith had not yet freed me. I had faith that God was real, but I was committed to a wrong perspective of God. The God I knew about was impersonal.

He "loved" me in only an obligatory sense, and He didn't really care about me enough to do anything meaningful with my life. I certainly did not feel loved by Him.

When I was younger, I believed I would always be successful. I was going to be a doctor, the president, or someone who could change the world, because that's what Mom said. Throughout high school, I made perfect grades and sat at the top of my class, setting me up for the full ride fellowship to the University of Arkansas I enjoyed as an undergrad.

According to Mom, I could have gone anywhere with my life.

Then Jesus grabbed hold of me in my freshman year of college. He set my heart on fire with love for Him, and in so doing, He reached out to me and somewhat narrowed my career options: He pointed my life in the direction of His glory.

It wasn't like I was a terrible person before Jesus did this. In fact, before Jesus rocked my world, I was a very good person—on the outside. It's just that, on the inside, I was not free. Like most in my generation, I walked in an addiction to things. For instance, before freedom, I was part of the slavery to pornography that is bleeding many in my generation dry. Before freedom, I was part of the slavery to sexual sin that is robbing my generation of its purity, emotional health, relational security, and ability to truly honor others. I lived for myself. My future, my goals, my talents, what I did when I was alone—all of it was focused on me and my gratification. My habits, my addictions, the things I committed my time to—all of it was glorifying to me. It was hedonism. A lack of conviction.

You might relate to some of this.

My life looked great on the outside, but on the inside, I was a slave to sin. I was a slave to greed, pride, and selfishness. I was a slave to lust and sexual impurity. I was very clean on the outside, not very clean on the inside. Jesus talked about this, once.

This lifestyle was bound for failure because I had no real integrity. The law of problems: if there is a problem, it will surface. When college came along, I fell. I crumbled and stepped into the most difficult time I have ever experienced. In that broken place, Christ stepped into my life in a loud way. (I'll get into those details later.)

Before my crash, I lived my life as I had because I didn't understand I belonged to God. He had been calling me His son ever since I called Him Lord in that boring church confirmation class, but I did not know it. I lived as a slave, in bondage to unholy things and unaware of the knowledge of how "for me" God really was. I lacked a revelation of my freedom in Christ. I did not know the power of grace in my life. I did not know the Father's heart toward me. So, I was bound by impure things.

The reality was, I was free in Christ and my identity was in Christ. But I threw chains around myself, preferring the cheap fruits of slavery to the unconquered fields of promised land.

> *O Lord, You have searched me and you know me. You know when I sit and when I rise; you perceive my thoughts from afar. You discern my going out and my lying down; you are familiar with all my ways. Before a word is on my tongue You know it completely, O Lord. You hem me in—behind and before; You have laid Your hand upon me. (Psalm 139:1-5, NIV1984)*

SONSHIP VS. SLAVERY

Only when we understand that the cross was the outpouring of God's heart for us and not an expression of His disgust with us can we really begin to see who God is and who we are in His eyes. We tend to let our sin identity stand as a filter between us and Jesus, allowing a mute idol to monitor and hinder our relationship with God. That isn't healthy.

God has called us to a greater, fuller relationship than that. He calls Himself greater than that, and He calls us, in Jesus, so much greater than that. He calls us to approach Him through the shed blood of Christ, but never through our sin. He calls us to move beyond our sin, and He calls us to see that our total depravity pales in comparison to our completed redemption.

Our redemption was finished at the cross. Now, through faith, we are children of God. We are no longer slaves to sin; we are members of a royal family.

> *But when the time had fully come, God sent his Son, born of a woman, born under law, to redeem those under law, that we might receive the full rights of sons. Because you are sons, God sent the Spirit of his Son into our hearts, the Spirit who calls out, 'Abba, Father.' So you are no longer a slave, but a son; and since you are a son, God has made you also an heir. (Galatians 4:4-7, NIV1984)*

As believers, we get to drop our slave mentalities and receive our adoption, our sonship. We actually get to receive our freedom.

The slave is totally depraved, but the son knows he is valued and has a place at the table. The slave sees in the cross only the bondage, condemnation, and judgment of sin, but the son sees in the cross the heart, love, and tender mercies of a good Father. The slave sees chains and tasks, but the son sees a future of freedom in an eternal Kingdom, as a product of grace. The slave allows guilt and shame to monitor his relationship with God, but the son knows he is mightily loved. The slave works desperately for his life, but the son walks in authority, dignity, and value, representing the Kingdom of his Father.

> *"Yet to all who received him, to those who believed in his name, he gave the right to become children of God..."*
> *(John 1:12)*

God spent Jesus's blood to call His people into a meaningful sonship, not to call wretches into shame and condemnation. He sacrificed Jesus to establish a royal priesthood that walks in the Father's mountain-moving love, not to gather a bunch of slaves bonded by fear and judgment under the banner of "depravity." The cross was never meant to keep us huddling around our sin, depravity, and shame. God's love and our shame are incompatible: one of the identities, son or wretch, has to go.

God gave us the cross so that we could step fully out of Egypt, walk through the desert, understand our identity, and arrive as His free children in promised land. Believing or living anything else will only bear fruit that falls short of what God has for our lives. A Christian life lived short of redemption and freedom is a life lived inaccurately.

MORE QUESTIONS

God loves us; the cross happened only because of this. Wrath was poured out only because God loves us. In His love for His creation, our Father poured out grace and wrath to free us from the sin that would keep us at a distance from Him. He is a good Father.

At the cross, He has redeemed us, and He has set us free. We are no longer slaves, but sons. We are no longer a kingdom of sinners, but a kingdom of royal priests under a holy King.

What if we quit defining ourselves by our depravity and stepped into the name "son" that God has spoken over us? What if we define ourselves the way the Father does, and quit assuming that we know better than He does? What if we built our faith on our Father's heart, and not on the lesser, defeated reality of our fallen state? What if we let God move us out from slavery and into sonship?

At the cross, the Father's love changed everything. The paradigm shifted. It is time we caught up to who we are in Christ.

We can't afford to settle for slavery because, in Christ, we are not slaves. We are sons, and we are free.

****

When looking back on an imperfect journey of faith, it is easy to be negative. It is easy to be dissatisfied and, therefore, dishonoring. For whatever reason, it is far easier in life to find things to be unhappy with than it is to find things worth celebrating. There is something in our flesh that makes bitterness an easy and familiar pathway to walk. But it does not have to be this way. We can choose to celebrate.

In this chapter, I have described my early Christian walk with less-than-sparkling words. Obviously, there are some things I would change about the various religious institutions, beliefs, and systems in which I grew up. However, I have come to praise God for them. I celebrate the foundation that was laid in me during those years. I celebrate the relationships and family I have there.

I would augment some things in my early faith environment, but the seeds that God planted in me during that season were exactly the seeds He needed to plant. That was a season of life every bit as orchestrated by God as the season of life I am currently in, and the seasons of God should not be despised. The seeds planted in me early on by those imperfect people, institutions, and programs were God's perfect seeds. They are the seeds responsible for the fruit my life is currently bearing.

Beautiful things grow up from imperfect, broken ground. The reality is, imperfect, broken ground is the only kind of ground with which God has to work. The only kind of people God has to work with are the imperfect, broken kind (including you and I). The only kind of institutions and beliefs that imperfect, broken people can build are the imperfect, broken kind.

None of us is truly qualified to represent the Father. None of us runs a perfect race. We choose to honor and celebrate the imperfect, faithful ones who have gone before us because we will only ever be the same for those who follow us. We do our best to obey and serve, and the Lord covers our broken best with His grace. Beautiful, free things grow up as a result.

CHAPTER 2

IN PRODIGAL LOVE

Every Christ-follower is personally aware of the kind of bondage the cross calls us *out of* (religion, sin, depression, addiction, anxiety, fallen condition, and more), but only a small fraction of believers actually experience the true and vibrant freedom the cross calls us *into*, through Christ.

The cross not only saves us *from* something, it saves us *into* something. It saves us *from* religious trying, and it saves us *into* secure relationship.

Only a small fraction of Christian believers ever make it out of the desert and into the life which God has called us. Very few ever make it out of slavery in Egypt, shed the slave mentality in the desert, and walk by faith through a miraculously dry riverbed into real freedom. A shocking few make it out of religion to arrive at relationship.

This book was inspired by the desire to help make that small number bigger.

As a future daddy, I am sometimes struck by the responsibility I will have to be a good father to my children. I get caught up in the weight of the responsibility of fatherhood, yet I don't even have a girlfriend. (I'm dramatic.) Fatherhood is kind of a big deal. It will be my job to be the kind of father who makes the Heavenly Father of Scripture palatable to my children. As their earthly father, if I give them a negative experience in life, there is a real possibility they will stumble over the truth of their good Father in Heaven. I know that if earthly fathers do nothing but hurt their children, those children may well expect only pain from their Heavenly Father. If their earthly father doesn't reward them, honor them, or remain faithful to them, their children may well expect that same belittling behavior from God, their Heavenly Father. If their earthly father consistently lies to them, lets them down, or abuses them, how much harder will those children find it to trust their eternal Father, whom they only know through faith? If I am not self-sacrificing for my children, who can expect them to understand the Father's self-sacrificing passion for us all at the cross?

I encounter these issues on a regular basis with the students I minister to and serve. Some students with broken family situations have no point of reference for what it means to have a good father. Many of them have never met their fathers. Many others have been abused by their fathers. (You might be one of them, or been part of a situation similar to theirs.) As a result, they have great difficulty understanding the heart of the good Father.

Fatherhood is a big responsibility. Many of the negative issues our society faces find their root in the problem of fatherlessness.

Growing up, my father was incredible. When I was younger, he forced me to do things I did not want to do because he had a perspective that was far less nearsighted than my own. As he made me do these things that I did not want to do, he saw me grow. In teaching me discipline, his wiser perspective saw me strengthened in the future, even while I experienced boredom and misery in the present. In teaching me commitment, his wiser perspective saw me matured later in my life, even while I experienced stress and stretching in the now. In teaching me to have integrity, his perspective saw me in the future, actually being who I claimed to be. He taught me many lessons. He saw qualities in me and about me that I could not possibly have seen, and he worked me hard so that I might grow into them.

Most important, though, was that he loved me—unconditionally. I know he would have hung on a cross for me, for the joy set before him: me.

The good news is, our Heavenly Father is the same way.

THE FATHER'S HEART

Jesus continued: 'There was a man who had two sons. The younger one said to his father, "Father, give me my share of the estate." So he divided his property between them.

Not long after that, the younger son got together all he had, set off for a distant country and there squandered his wealth in wild living. After he had spent everything, there was a severe famine in that whole country, and he began to be in need. So he went and hired himself out to a citizen of that country, who sent him to his fields to feed pigs. He longed to fill his stomach with the pods that the pigs were eating, but no one gave him anything.

When he came to his senses, he said, "How many of my father's hired men have food to spare, and here I am starving to death! I will set out and go back to my father and say to him: Father, I have sinned against heaven and against you. I am no longer worthy to be called your son; make me like one of your hired men." So he got up and went to his father.

But while he was still a long way off, his father saw him and was filled with compassion for him; he ran to his son, threw his arms around him and kissed him.

The son said to him, "Father, I have sinned against heaven and against you. I am no longer worthy to be called your son." But the father said to his servants, "Quick! Bring the best robe and put it on him. Put a ring on his finger and sandals on his feet. Bring the fattened calf and kill it. Let's have a feast and celebrate. For this son of mine was dead and is alive again; he was lost and is found." So they began to celebrate.

Meanwhile, the older son was in the field. When he came near the house, he heard music and dancing. So he called one of the servants and asked him what was going on. "Your brother has come," he replied, "and your father has killed the fattened calf because he has him back safe and sound."

The older brother became angry and refused to go in. So his father went out and pleaded with him. But he answered his father, "Look! All these years I've been slaving for you and never disobeyed your orders. Yet you never gave me even a young goat so I could celebrate with my friends. But when this son of yours who has squandered your property with prostitutes comes home, you kill the fattened calf for him!"

"My son," the father said, "you are always with me, and everything I have is yours. But we had to celebrate and be glad, because this brother of yours was dead and is alive again; he was lost and is found." (Luke 15:11-32)

****

The moral of this story: No matter what you have squandered, no matter how much you have sinned against the Father and Heaven, no matter how far you have run, and no matter how unworthy you feel to be His child, God wants to lavish His mercies on you. God wants His lost and broken child back. This is the Father's heart.

What, then, shall we say in response to this? If God is for us, who can be against us? He who did not spare his own Son, but gave him up for us all—how will he not also, along with him, graciously give us all things? Who will bring any charge against those whom God has chosen? It is God who justifies. Who is he that condemns? Christ Jesus, who

*dies—more than that, who was raised to life—is at the
right hand of God and is also interceding for us. Who shall
separate us from the love of Christ?*

(Romans 8:31-35, NIV1984)

*The Lord your God is with you, he is mighty to save. He will
take great delight in you, he will quiet you with his love, he
will rejoice over you with singing.*

(Zephaniah 3:17, NIV1984)

MISSING GRACE

Entire libraries of books have been written on the parable of the lost son, and I don't intend to do that here. I'll simply survey the characters in the story in order to shed some light on the heart of the Father.

The older brother/son. This first character—the eldest son—was a prototype Pharisee. In his sad misunderstanding of a proper father-son relationship, he missed out on the simplest and most glorious treasure of all: nearness to his father.

This guy represents those of us in the Church who simply do not understand God's grace. He represents a religious crowd that believes it is entitled to the love and gifts of the Father, by virtue of dutiful and religious working. The older brother represents the hearts of those of us in the Church who have deceived ourselves into thinking we have earned our relationship with God by "doing" and "building" for Him. He represents those who have missed out on the blessings of simply "being" and "loving." He represents those in the faith who are embittered by the "lost sons" who have returned to the Father, aware of their need for His grace.

The dude didn't get it. He worked, strove, and contended for his father's approval, completely missing the fact that his father's love was already entirely his. He thought he had earned his standing with his father. He didn't realize, in his arrogant and foolish sense of entitlement, that his position and provision were due only to his father's grace and love. His striving for his father's love was unnecessary. It was already completely and totally his.

The older brother depicts someone strongly influenced by a religious spirit. Just as he believed that his faithful work for his father entitled him to his father's grace and love, it is clear from his response to his brother's return that he also believed sin or disobedience should disqualify him from his father's grace and love. He worked to earn favor, and he believed failure to perform would lose it. That's called "religion." Otherwise known as "bondage."

The moment we believe that our relationship with God is contingent upon our performance (good or bad), we have bought into the lie of religion and have set ourselves up for a lot of failure and pain.

Covenant love (the Father's heart) and our covenant relationship with the Father have nothing to do with us or our ability to perform, morally. They have everything to do with the Father's ability to maintain our relationship, even in the midst of our foolishness. Covenant relationship is absolutely freeing.

The sad thing about the older son (and real-life people like him) is that he was so caught up in his jealousy and entitlement to the favor of his father that he couldn't bring himself to celebrate the return of his little brother. He did not celebrate, and he certainly was not glad at the return of one whom he should have dearly loved. It is likely the older brother felt no sorrow at his younger brother's leaving in the first place. The older brother clearly did not prevent his younger brother from leaving, and he certainly did not snatch him from his rebellion.

The older brother's sense of entitlement to his standing absolutely distracted him from his love for his little brother. Pride, jealousy, and religion were the key components. What it boils down to is, in his failure to understand his own need for his father's grace, the older brother failed to love. We can learn from his failure.

For this character, however, there is much hope! In explaining the celebration of the younger son's return to the oldest son, the father is tender and patient. He didn't revoke his love for his oldest son out of disappointment or condemnation, as a lesser father might have. The father wasn't ashamed of his son's religious spirit, rather, he continues to love him, despite his son's foolishness. Even after his son's arrogance and ignorance are exposed, his father invited the son to join in with the household in celebration. Just as lost in his pride, entitlement, and jealousy as his younger brother ever had been in a faraway land, the older brother was also pursued by the father. It was in the father's heart to pursue the foolish older son, regardless of his refusal to enter into the household's joy.

Our Father has a heart of relentless pursuit.

****

When I was a kid growing up, my brother and I did not get along. In fact, I would venture to say we were probably each other's least favorite person alive. That sounds extreme, but it is close to being true. We were extremely competitive and jealous for our parents' attention and affection.

We were nothing alike. And each of us clearly wanted to be a little bit more like the other. We were jealous of one another's gifts, talents, abilities, friends, girlfriends, cars, and more. It was a no-holds-barred type jealousy, and it led to a lot of bitterness and general frustration. We argued a lot, cussed a lot, threatened a lot, and yelled a lot. When Mom and Dad weren't around, things were typically messy.

One vivid memory: One day, I called my brother an idiot, pushed some buttons, and pointed out to him how smart I was. This made him angry, so he ran at me, intent on beating me up, I think. I'm pretty sure he was going to punch me in the face. I ran the opposite direction to my bedroom and locked the door. He yelled at me and called me rude things that I deserved to be called. Then, unable to punch me, he punched my door. To this day, there is a hole in my bedroom door at home. I think we told Mom and Dad that we were moving furniture or something, but I don't think they believed us. (You can only try.) We were teenagers.

Anyway, so much of our bitterness, enmity, and borderline hatred toward each other were due to the absolutely false beliefs we had that led us to compete with each other for our self-worth. Our competition was an extremely ridiculous source of conflict, looking at it from this end of adolescence. Now, we can see clearly that our parents loved each of us enormously. Our conflicts were absurd. There was more than enough love and worth to go around.

Our rivalry was ridiculous, but it provides an important picture, relevant to so many peoples' relationships with God.

How ridiculous it is that we, the sons and daughters of God, compete for the favor of the Father—as if there isn't enough to go around! How ridiculous is our envy, bitterness, and competition for the favor of God and the people around us? How ridiculous is our covetousness? How impeded is our love for others by our absolutely false ideas that we could ever earn, compete for, or hold a monopoly on our Father's love for us?

We would benefit from a proper understanding of the Father. He is a God of abundance. In His Kingdom, there is never lack.

I think, for the religious, this is an extremely significant issue. As the religious leave spiritual adolescence—just as my brother and I left ours—I believe we will be exposed to the absurdity of our efforts to battle each other, battle sin, or battle through life for God's love.

Why punch holes in doors when the Father's love is freely available to be enjoyed?

"It is finished."

NEEDING GRACE

The younger brother/son. This is the well-known "lost" or "prodigal" son. This guy is pretty famous. I believe the parable of the lost son is more about the heart of the father than it is about any of the characters, but the younger son typically steals the stage in teachings on this story.

After all, at face value, this character *is* the character to which all believers in Christ are supposed to relate. All of us are born into prodigal life, through Adam. All of us are in desperate need of the Father's grace in order to be restored to our intended identity of sonship.

The younger son's rebellion reflects many of our journeys very well. He rejected the father's authority, went away with the father's goodies, wasted the father's goodies, and ended up starving and desperate, separated from his father's protective covering. In the midst of his rebellion against his father, he eventually came to realize how much he needed him. In light of his recklessness and sin, he judged himself unworthy of sonship under his father, but he returned home anyway (hungry and ashamed), willing to be provided for as a mere servant in his father's house.

The main role of the younger son in the story is to display the father's reckless love for his son, despite the son's rebellious journey, during which he did anything but earn the love of his father.

When most people read this parable, they differentiate between the younger and older sons. The truth is, however, that the two brothers are more alike than they are different. They have the same religious spirit. The younger son has the same religious spirit as the older son, but his religious attitude manifests itself differently. While the older son was a broken and lost individual because of his pride, the younger son was a broken and lost individual because of his shame. The older son believed, falsely, that he was near to his father because he had it all together. The younger son believed, falsely, that his rebellion against his father had terminated his sonship, and that he would have to grovel in shame to earn a place back at the estate. Both were spiritually crushed by the manifestations of religion (shame and entitlement), because both believed that their father's love for them depended on them and their capabilities. They were wrong.

Religious-spiritedness is a coin. On one side of the coin are pride and entitlement, and on the other side are shame and disgrace. No matter which way the coin lands, there is bad news and a false interpretation of the Father's heart. In their religion, both sons missed out on knowing the Father's heart.

The prodigal son, just like the older son, was sold out to the belief that his relationship with his father was all about his ability to behave. He believed his relationship to be ruined irreparably because of his brokenness and disobedience. The younger son had failed to perform, so he thought this canceled his sonship. At the very least, he saw intimacy with his father as an impossibility. Surely, he believed his father would be ashamed of him.

He couldn't have been further from the truth.

Where so many believers today go wrong is in the false belief that they are supposed to embody the shame of the younger son. This is a big problem because "younger son" shame masquerades as humility wherever religion reigns. However, the shame of the younger son was not humility. It is shame, and shame is deadly to a person's identity. Notice how he devalued himself and groveled. His was a countenance born of shame, and it prevented him from operating in his sonship. Still, many embrace the younger son's attitude and mistake it for humility. They fail to realize they are actually stunting themselves, keeping themselves from the fruits of sonship and intimacy with God.

The cross simply does not call us into shame or disgrace. The cross does not call us *into* a humility based on our short-fallings. The cross calls us *out from* all that. Though the younger son's shame and disgrace are real, as redeemed believers we are not to identify with them.

Instead, we are to embrace the father's response to his son's shame: grace, favor, mercy, sacrifice, and a new proclamation of sonship. It is God's response to our shame, not merely our shame, which should define our humility and our faith.

The difference between false humility (shame or insecurity) and humility is critical. Shame says, "You are worthless," "You are dirty," or "You blew it all in your sin and rebellion." Humility says, "God loves me in a way that I don't deserve," "God's mercies are new each morning," and "My sin is real, but my God is more real." False humility will devalue you. True humility will exalt God. False humility puts a pitiful you at the center of things. True humility puts a holy God at the center of things. Humility isn't about devaluing self; it's about exalting God.

HUMBLE HEART

We need to make a distinction between the shame of the lost son and the humbled, repentant heart of the lost son. The father ignored the shame of the prodigal son, but he embraced his repentance and humility.

This story might have ended differently had the lost son returned to the father in pride, as if entitled to the grace of the father. But he returned with neither pride nor entitlement. He returned very sorry, very repentant, and knowing he had very foolishly done wrong against his father and against Heaven. He returned with much shame, yes, but he also returned with a heart to change his ways and obey. We are called to have this kind of heart of repentance, to have a broken heart that understands we can and should do better.

This call to repentance is *never* a call to walk in shame. If it were, it would be a call to chains. Jesus says, "Repent," but He never calls His image bearers to walk in shame. Shame has never been in God's image. When Jesus said, "Repent, and turn from your sins," He called us to distance ourselves from our shame, not to continue walking in it.

The lost son's humble repentance became crippling shame when he allowed his rebellion to define him. This is critical. The son could only aspire to be a slave after his identity in shame was established. There is no freedom in identifying with our rebellions. It leads us nowhere but back to rebellion. It is why Christ gave us new identities.

All that said, this parable isn't really about the younger son's shame; it's about the grace of the father in response to the son's shame. The story of the prodigal son is not about how the younger son sees himself; it's about how the father sees him. It's about how the father's love enabled the son to return from rebellion and step into a legitimate sonship that had never actually ceased. In this parable, we are called away from the idea that the Father would ever demote or revoke His love for us in our shame.

In disgust at his own sin, the younger son thought himself disqualified from right standing with his own father. He took it upon himself to believe the falsehood that he was no longer worthy of his father's love. However, as the father made clear upon his younger son's arrival back home, it was never really up to him to determine an end to the love he would receive from his father.

Fact: It is never up to us to determine an end to the love we receive from the Father.

By story's end, the father has corrected the son's shame and reinstated him to his proper place of sonship. The father replaced his younger son's own flawed opinion of himself with truth born only of God the Father's heart. He erased the son's ambition for servanthood and slavery and reestablished his sonship. With the sacrifice of the fattened calf, the father covered all the lies the younger son had bought into about the end of his father's love. The father rejoiced over his son with celebration. The younger son was removed from a misinformed place of unworthiness and groveling for servanthood and placed back on his feet by the father's love—new robes, new ring, renewed confidence.

> *For this is what the Sovereign Lord says: I myself will search for my sheep and look after them. As a shepherd looks after his scattered flock when he is with them, so will I look after my sheep. I will rescue them from all the places where they were scattered on a day of clouds and darkness... I will search for the lost and bring back the strays. I will bind up the injured and strengthen the weak, but the sleek and strong I will destroy. I will shepherd the flock with justice. (Ezekiel 34:11-16)*

****

Even if I wanted to, I couldn't possibly stop being my parents' child. I could disown them, and they could disown me, but the fact remains that we are biologically related. Until the day I receive my resurrection body, genetically, I will remain in the image of my mother and father. We are relatives because of the blood we share.

I could offend my parents. I could dishonor them. I could disobey them. I could completely disregard them. I could treat them with scorn. Right this moment, I could demand from them my rightful inheritance. I could publicly denounce them. I could cast off their authority over my life, and I could run away from them in rebellion.

However, there is one thing I cannot do: I cannot stop being their child. I cannot end that blood relationship. If they desire to love me, I cannot keep them from loving me. Love is powerful. It is enduring, and it holds a ton of weight. Who am I to deny that I am my parents' child? Who am I to determine their love for me? Those are not decisions I get to make. My mother's and father's love for me is not up to me.

My Father's love for me is not up to me. I am His son, because He gave me His blood.

I was such a brat when I was young. I really was. I remember, on multiple occasions, screaming at my mother, "I hate you!" Most of the time, I'd say that immediately after having been placed in time-out. I knew "I hate you" would hurt my mom, so I used those words to manipulate her feelings in attempts to get what I wanted. I remember sitting with my nose in the time-out corner, screaming that at my mom, over her tears.

"I hate you" cut her to her core. She cried. It was awful.

However, no matter how much I intentionally hurt my mom in those immature little temper tantrums, her love for me prevailed. In those moments, I'm sure she was convinced that I wanted nothing to do with her (even though I didn't understand or mean what I said). I'm sure she thought she was a terrible mother. I'm sure she felt like a total failure as a parent. I'm sure it hurt. I'm sure that her heart bled in the measure to which she loved me, which means, she bled a lot.

Try as I might, I couldn't stop her love for me—not even when I wanted to. Not even when I ignorantly valued other things more than her. She loved me, though I didn't deserve it, though she could have chosen to do otherwise.

Just like God.

(Sorry, Mom.)

****

In the parable of the lost son, a fattened calf was slaughtered to celebrate the return of the lost son to the family. Today, we can easily see the foreshadowing of Jesus's death in the slaughtered calf. We can actually see God's hand in the parable. Not only was the father celebrating his son, but he was also "restoring" his son to sonship. The blood of the fattened calf "cleansed" him of his shame.

What can be difficult for us to see is the application of this parable in our own lives, in terms of the Father's love toward us today. Christians in my generation struggle to see the grace of our Heavenly Father and His delight at our own return to Him, regardless of our own rebellious journeys. We struggle due to either religious entitlement or shame and disgrace. We believe the lie and it causes us to resist the truth that the Father's heart is freely for us today, regardless of how much we think we have to earn His love—regardless of how far we have tried to run from Him. As a result of believing this way, we walk around in pride or in shame, separating ourselves from the Father's heart.

> *And you have forgotten that word of encouragement that addresses you as sons: 'My son, do not make light of the Lord's discipline, and do not lose heart when he rebukes you, because the Lord disciplines those he loves, and he punishes everyone he accepts as a son.' Endure hardship as discipline; God is treating you as sons. For what son is not disciplined by his father?*
>
> *(Hebrews 12:5-7, NIV1984)*

GIVING GRACE

This generation of Christians can choose to be one of three people from this story. We can choose to be the "older son," enslaved by our own religious entitlements and duties, blind to our need for grace, and unable to rejoice over the return of our own brothers and sisters. Alternatively, we can choose to be the "prodigal son," buried by our own shame and disgrace, seeking only servanthood and settling for unworthiness, regardless of the *blood* that makes us our Father's sons and daughters. Finally, we can choose to be the "reinstated son" and see our Father celebrating our return, declaring us worthy of sonship, regardless of the shame we would have carried. The sonship we choose will be determined by what we believe about our Father's heart. What we believe about the Father's heart will determine what we believe about ourselves.

If we incorrectly believe that the Father's love can be earned, or that He is obligated to reward religious success, we will forever be hopeless "older sons." If we incorrectly believe that the Father's heart will turn from us in our shame, or that He revokes His love from those who run from Him, we will forever be hopeless "prodigal sons." However, if we understand that the Father's heart is freely available to those broken ones who know they need His grace, we will step into the freedom He has for us.

> *'Is not Ephraim my dear son, the child in whom I delight?*
> *Though I often speak against him, I still remember him.*
> *Therefore my heart yearns for him; I have great compas-*
> *sion for him,' declares the Lord. (Jeremiah 31:20)*

****

My generation is really interesting. We crave authenticity. We are not satisfied with smoke and mirrors, and something in us instantly questions the authority of all the made-up faces we see on TV.

We grew up in a time of a great trust deficit, a time when all the leaders around us fell morally and dramatically. Enron, any number of politicians or presidents, Freddie Mac, Fannie Mae, Lehman Brothers, the rest of Wall Street, athletic superstars, church leaders, teachers, coaches, music and entertainment icons, and more.

All around us, from every angle and from every pillar, so many fell. They failed to live up to the image that they had worked so hard to portray to the world.

Top-heavy, when given a little push, they tumbled. Down they went, and with them, our trust. Trust deficit.

Furthermore, far too many in my generation have watched their families fall apart. We grew up in an age of broken marriages, an age when we actually began to expect covenants to be broken the moment they became inconvenient or expensive. The most recent statistic I heard was that 60 percent of all new marriages will end in divorce.

Why trust anything less than covenant if you can't trust covenant? Trust deficit.

Society is falling. Really, it has fallen. The world we grew up in was ridden with character flaws, diseases, and a lack of desire to fix the problems. The law of problems, again: if there is a problem, it will surface.

Just as my generation craves authenticity, we crave integrity. We crave a time and place when peoples' grand words and visions spring from the overflow of their hearts, and not from attempts to create a following or electorate. We crave someone who lives his or her life with conviction. We crave leaders who will stand on truth, unwilling to compromise to the relativistic society we live in. Honestly, at this point, we're thirsty just to see leaders who are willing to stand on anything, truth or not, without wavering and without falling.

We crave what is genuine. We crave transparency, and we crave satisfaction with what we will find underneath the transparent, unashamed surface. We crave a lot.

We crave a lot because we have been promised a lot, only to be let down a lot. We have tasted a vision, only to have that vision pulled out from under us by the strings that were attached to it. Thus, our cynicism.

As far as we are into the age of trust deficit, there is still hope. We can trust the Father. We have to trust the Father. And we have to build our institutions and culture on His heart. We can't really wrap our minds around it by using our experiences in this world as points of reference, but we can trust our Father.

What's my point? We struggle with trust deficit, but if the Father says He loves us, let's trust Him. If the Father has called us sons, let's trust that He wants this to be a meaningful relationship. If the Father is calling us to step out of our chains and into freedom, let's not hesitate. I think some of our generation's refusal to move forward in our freedom is based in our inability to trust the Father.

Our task is to somehow turn over to the Father our own opinions of our worth, value, and purpose. In our limited perspectives, and in our fallen perceptions, we cannot help but craft a broken and stained image of ourselves. We are bound to fall short of the glory of God, even in our own opinions of ourselves. We need a greater opinion; we need a judge. We need to trust what the Father is saying over us. Valuing our opinions over His is a dangerous thing.

If He says we are free, we are free.

****

For the most part, members of my generation are well acquainted with our brokenness. Integrity is a value that seems to be surging among believers my age. We seek authenticity, and anything short of that is a waste of time. Thus, the believers of my generation tend to acknowledge that we are far from perfect, and we have an intense knowledge of our own need for God's grace (so intense that it can easily become shame). One thing we have a pretty good handle on is that we know, in our heads, that we can't earn the Father's love.

I am not concerned that my generation will embrace the type of sonship that believes the Father's heart must be earned and maintained by constant effort (though concerning people, religious pride will always be an issue). I believe the much more pressing issue for our younger demographic of the Church is shame. It's the other side of the religious spirit "coin." It's why I have written this book.

Believers in my generation experience so much "lost son" shame. We know we are undoubtedly saved by the grace of God, but we swim around in our shame. We waste time in imaginary chains. We are free, but our shame and perceived worthlessness keep us from ever leaving our Egypt. Because of the cross, our chains have actually fallen away, but we have chosen to remain slaves to our shame and disgrace. Like the prodigal son, we settle for unworthiness and servanthood, despite the *blood* Christ shed to usher in the great love and relationship offered by God's heart.

Many of God's people are kept in disgrace by our tendency to identify with our rebellion rather than with Christ. In that identity, we have determined that we are incompatible with God's love and that He cannot love us out of our shame. Like the prodigal son, we have an inaccurate view of the Father's heart for us, and therefore, we walk as if we are not sons. Like the prodigal son, many of us have, in effect, wrongly disqualified ourselves from the heart of the Father, and we seek merely to do lowly tasks in the Father's house.

Here is the Good News: the Father's heart beats for us, His children, whether we give it our permission to or not.

As a people that is being called out of shame and into freedom, we need to understand God's love is *for* us. Just as the father's love was *for* his "lost son" in lavish ways, the love of God is *for* us in lavish ways. This sets us free. Until we step into this lavish freedom, we underutilize our lives here on the earth.

REDEEMED

The third type of sonship—the sonship our Father calls us to—is the sonship that experiences the delight and celebration of the Father. It's the sonship of freedom. It's redemption.

In the parable, the father sees his returning prodigal son from a distance, is filled with compassion, and actually runs out to meet him before he is able to complete his journey home. The father wraps his arms around his son and kisses him before he even gets a chance to express his shame.

The father was no fool in letting his son leave and giving him the means to rebel. In fact, he was wise in doing so. The father probably knew that the son would come to realize his need for the father's covering, but it was always up to the son to return to his father. The father let the son learn firsthand his need for him, and he rejoiced when his son came back, acknowledging his foolish rebellion.

(I can only imagine the pain in the father's heart as the prodigal son was ruining himself, out from under the protection and covering of the father. Talk about learning something the hard way!)

When the son returned, repentant and humbled by his need for his father, the father dismissed the son's claim to shame and demanded a celebration. He clothed his son with his best robe, and he put a signet ring back on his son's finger. He sacrificed the fattened calf and threw a feast.

The father rejoiced over his son's new life.

Did the "lost son" deserve any of this? No. Was he guilty of his sin? Yeah.

Did the Father comply with our opinions and perceptions of guilt and worth? No, praise God. When we return to Him in true repentance and humility, the Father's response to our guilt and shame is *always* reckless grace. The Father ignored the son's shame, covered his rebellion with a blood sacrifice, and called him "son" again. Such grace. Such love.

That's the kind of sonship that leads to freedom. Sonship based on grace, love, and the Father's opinion of our worth. Sonship based on the *Father's* redeeming blood sacrifice, the *Father's* finest robes, and the *Father's* wide-open arms. Any other interpretation of the Christian faith—any kind of faith contingent upon anything but the Father's identity for us—falls short of security and liberty.

God is calling us to be His sons, free from entitlement, shame, and sin-centeredness. "Oldest son" religion and "lost son" shame both leave us empty. Only a proper understanding of our Father's heart will lead us to a proper sonship. We can't afford to build our relationship with the Father upon our ability to avoid sin, and we can't afford to have our relationship with the Father crippled by shame.

We are called to a sonship founded on *God's heart*, and nothing else. We are to understand that we have the Father's heart only because God is in the business of loving us. We can't earn His heart, and we can't run from His heart. We just have to receive it. Enter prodigal love.

CHAPTER 3

THE HOT AND DRY PLACES

Pain, tragedy, and crisis can direct our steps far more consistently than the life, promises, and hope found in Jesus Christ. Fear and darkness can tend to motivate us rather than light and truth. For some, depression and dry seasons not only dominate the past, but reach into the present as well, wreaking havoc on the joy and seasons of fruitfulness God has ready for us.

We are a generation under attack—a generation addicted to artificial joy, willing to bow its head to things inferior to God, leading to a joy inferior to His. We are a generation that must learn to contend for our faith in Christ, our joy.

If you are a believer in Christ, your past and your shame have already been conquered at the cross. In the present, you get to stand in judgment over your past, and you get to rewrite it. You have an editor. In Jesus, you get to reconsider your story, and you get to claim a new identity and new promises.

What Satan calls misery in your life, Jesus calls your ministry and your mission field. Your past is in the grave, and Jesus is dancing all over it. At the cross, your entire life was redeemed. The moment Jesus died to set you free from your past, you became free from it.

Consider yourself encouraged.

You have probably heard something along these lines: "It was easy for God to get the Israelites out of Egypt, but it took forty years in the desert to get Egypt out of the Israelites." The fact is, the moment God broke Egypt's bondage over Israel, Israel became free. However, for nearly four decades, Israel wandered the desert under Moses's leadership with a slave mentality. Israel remained in bondage to its past (and understandably so, having been a nation in chains for centuries). The people of Israel carried bondage with them into their new, meaningful freedom. The religious spirit was at work in the desert.

I think many of us are a lot like Israel.

In their desert season, God's chosen people cycled continuously through different phases of doubting God's power, word, faithfulness, goodness, leadership, and provision. Although they were led, visibly, by the presence of their deliverer Himself (by pillars of cloud and fire), they behaved as if they were still slaves. They acted as if they were still under the yoke of a wicked king, still in bondage to a master they couldn't trust, and still in service to a powerless kingdom of darkness. They didn't trust Him, they didn't want to obey Him, and they didn't follow Him with joy. They had no idea who they were.

Basically, they didn't take God at His word when He said, "You, Israel, are free, and you are mine." So they wandered, their faith unready for the Promised Land.

I think much of the religious pain people suffer today stems from that same reality. We haven't fully grasped the truth of God's words: "You, child, are free, and you are mine." We have no idea who we are. So we wander, our faith unready for promised land.

We remain God's people in the desert, in bondage to our past, waiting for God to do something special in order to prove Himself to us. All the while, God is waiting for us to realize, by faith, that He has already done something special. He has already set us free.

The generation of Israelites that had been slaves in Egypt actually had to die off before God would take His nation, Israel, into the Promised Land. The group of bitter, complaining, ashamed, doubting, faithless, and damaged former slaves wasn't about to inherit God's promise. They had no idea who they really were, so they were not ready for the destiny God had for them. They died and were buried just short of the Promised Land.

Chances are, you are going to have to let a significant part of yourself die. You are going to have to bury that part of who you *were* that presently holds you from your future. You will have to leave your old body and your old identity in the desert in order to move into God's promises for your life.

God did it for Israel, and He will do it for you. It is time we step across the river into real liberty. Don't be afraid to leave who you were behind.

MY DESERT

My sophomore year in college, and the summers that bookended it, were characterized by some pretty extreme depression. In my desert, I isolated myself, wrecked some of my closest friendships, and thought a lot about death. I had convinced myself that I wasn't loved, that I was alone, and that I was worthless.

These were lies, of course, but I believed them. I walked in a bizarre kind of isolation that didn't end, even when I was with the people I was supposed to love and be loved by most. For the better part of a year, I felt (I *knew*) that I was totally alone, and that no one really cared.

It hurt. A lot. There was no joy or peace in that place.

Today, I look back at that depression and am totally puzzled. The entire season was irrational, emotional, and reckless. It was a deeply inward conflict (one throughout which the Father was faithfully present), and the lordship in my life was contested.

In that season, I saw all my sin and my shame, and its disgust-ingness defined me. I was a believer in God at that time, but the last thing I understood or knew was the Father's love and grace for *me*. I was hollow. I saw my broken relationships and began to believe a lie that said all I was capable of was broken relation-ships. I *believed* that I was alone and unloved, and that nothing could change this. I believed God was not *for* me, but had dropped me off to leave me in my shame and depression.

Lies? Yes. However, I believed them because they fit the pain I was experiencing. (Never believe something only because it matches your experience. Believe truth, regardless of your expe-rience, and your experience will come into alignment with truth.) Satan did a great job on me. He knew exactly where to throw his punches.

****

Church moment: Raise your hand if you know that death is a ter-rifying prospect for those who lack a revelation of the Kingdom of God. About two years ago, I began to experience that fear of death. Death terrified me because I was considering suicide and because I had no revelation of the eternal Kingdom of God. (Granted, if I had known then what I know now about God's Kingdom, I wouldn't have been depressed.) Terrified of what death might look like, I didn't commit suicide (obviously).

These days, nothing breaks my heart more than to hear that someone in my group of friends, or in my ministry, is battling thoughts of suicide. It hurts, because I've been there, and something in their struggle resonates within me.

If you have never experienced depression to the extent that you want to kill yourself, I can tell you that it is not a state of mind to be desired. The truth is, everyone has walked through various cycles and levels of shame and depression. This may vary in frequency and magnitude from person to person, but shame and depression are universal human experiences (because sin is a universal human experience). It's just that many people fail to recognize or express their shame and depression.

There are certainly physiological causes for most of what we call "depression," but it is important to remember that everything mental, physical, or emotional that we experience has unseen, spiritual roots.

The "good" things we experience mentally, physically, or emotionally have unseen roots that tap into the blessings of God. The things we experience that fall short of God's standard of "very good" in our bodies, minds, and hearts, however, have deep roots into something else—something far short of God's glory.

God did not place us in a system wherein depression was a part of His plan. Depression happens when something in our minds causes our thoughts to self-destruct inwardly and angrily, and our joy escapes us. Depression, like most mental illness, is an inward battle. It is not of God. A lack of joy in the very heart of who you are is a dark thing.

For the most part, our depression arises from our failure to drive deep roots into the Kingdom of God—the Kingdom that brings hope, peace, and joy. Without our inner life driven deeply into the Kingdom, we are vulnerable to winds and waves of dark thoughts. We float in them, away from our anchor, and they beat the heck out of us. The inward chaos and self-loathing of depression are toxic. When you start believing Satan's lies and claim them as your own identity, you are bound to crash and burn.

Fortunately, no conflict is so inward or isolating as to happen beyond the reach, presence, and friendship of God. In that stormy place of darkness, Jesus is patiently present, walking on the roiling seas. The Father rests, waiting for us to realize that our problem is not as desperate as we think it is. He is there, ready to help us filter, sort, and process our inward conflicts. God is as much a healer now in the inner, solitary world of our minds as He was when He walked the streets of Capernaum. It is in the supernatural resolution of our inner chaos that we learn what it really means, that the God of all peace resides within us. When we introspect in our despair, we must understand we are especially poised to encounter the Christ in us. From that encounter on, we come to know and respond to the friend who is intimately near to us in any kind of darkness.

Nothing in the world made me feel worse than the lies I believed: I am absolutely nasty, my sins are unredeemable, I will never be forgiven for all I've done. All these lies are derivative of the same lie: The sins you've committed establish your value and your identity. Your value is in your sin; therefore, you are disgusting. Your eternal worth amounts to pain, shame, and flames .

Lies and tears. You get the picture. It was a nasty place to be.

Depression is a chain, and chains are made out of darkness. As such, they go away when you shine some light on them. Public service announcement: If you know someone who is walking in depression, do not take it lightly. They are walking through hell. The good news is, you can pour living water all over their situation. You are on the outside, but it is possible to help them through their struggle. Help them, and help them get help.

****

My desert season lasted over a year, and it totally wrecked my sophomore year of college. (Yes, it could have been much worse.) However, now I am *free*. Forever. I am on the other side of the river from the desert, having taken leaps and bounds into promised land.

You will have to take my word for this, but like so many of you, I am no stranger to pain. I have a rich understanding of what it means to walk through the valley of the shadow of death. I share my story not to be dramatic or to provoke pity, but to say that I have a testimony of deliverance. I can tell you that, at your realization of God's love for you, and by God's hand, your desert will come to an end. You will find joy when you discover exactly who it is that you are: a child of the King. God's promises will punch through the lies that chain you down, and your thirst will be met. Your identity in Christ will set you free.

> *When Israel was a child, I loved him, and out of Egypt I called my son. But the more I called Israel, the further they went from me....It was I who taught Ephraim to walk, taking them by the arms; but they did not realize it was I who healed them. I led them with cords of human kindness, with ties of love; I lifted the yoke from their neck and bent down to feed them. (Hosea 11:1-4, NIV1984)*

GOOD AND BAD

There are two kinds of deserts: the good kind and the bad kind. Praise God, He redeems even the bad ones for His and His children's good.

There is nothing intrinsically evil about the concept of a desert. In fact, I could argue that all desert seasons are actually brought about by our Father. Deserts are a biblical theme. They represent the dry seasons in our life that God leads us into for the purpose of strengthening, refining, or growing us. He tends to put us in hard places where there is nothing to depend on but Him so that we can't help but learn to depend on Him. Desert seasons tend to be transitional seasons for us.

We are sent into deserts to be tested. God leads us into hot, dry places with His Spirit in order to test our identity. These seasons always precede fruitfulness in Kingdom work.

While most deserts are overwhelmingly good for us, some deserts turn sour when we, like Israel during its exodus, miss the boat out of the desert and remain in our slave mentality far longer than God ever intended. They turn bad when we, like Israel, fail the test of walking into our God-given identity. Satan enters the desert and does his best to twist something that is very good for us into something that is very bad for us. With our unredeemed slave mentality intact, the shame and chains from our season of bondage in Egypt follow us into the desert. Shame, lies, and chains, which are actually broken in our deliverance from Egypt, keep us wandering in the desert until we accept the revelation of our Father's heart (or until we die, as Israel did).

This "slave's mentality" is a problem for my generation. We walk *into* the desert freed, but walk *through* the desert thinking and acting as if we are still slaves to whatever former master in Egypt that held us back from our destiny. In light of the liberty God promises us, our self-imposed slavery is ridiculous.

Deserts are crucial seasons in our lives when initiated by the love of God. Tough spots to begin with, deserts turn nasty when the effects of sin come in to taint God's plan. Often, sin, shame, and guilt come in to anchor us in the hot and dry places. When our shame keeps us in the desert, even after the Father's love has led us to the way out, good deserts turn bad. We are starving our destinies by remaining in the desert, when, by God's grace, we could already be in promised land. For this reason, it is important that we pass the identity test in the desert.

One of the most difficult things for any believer to grasp is that God sends us into difficulty. Our good Father sends us into brokenness. God prepares for us deserts and pain, and He prepares us for them. This is difficult to grasp because it's hard to understand why our good Father would want to wound His children. We ask, "Why would our good Father want His child broken, miserable, or in a difficult place?" It's easy to imagine that the enemy wants us stuck in a desert. It is much more difficult, however, to imagine that our Heavenly Father would want this. So we must ask, why would God want us in a desert?

Our Father leads us into deserts because He wants us weak. He wants us weak because He wants us to experience His strength. When we are weakest in life, He is strongest in us. It is when Christ is strongest in us that we can best see our identity in Him. When we finally understand our identity in Him, we can be sent into promised land.

Satan wants us in deserts so that we might be destroyed. The Father wants us in deserts so that we might become powerful. Our response to our weakness in the desert will determine which end we will experience.

Jesus was led into the desert by the Spirit of God. He left the desert, after enduring Satan's tests, by the power of the Spirit of God. Being led somewhere *by the Spirit* and walking from somewhere *by the power of the Spirit* are two very different things! One takes us to the mountain. The other gives us power to move the mountain. It is God's will for our lives that we endure deserts so that we will come out of them by the power of His Spirit. It is only after these desert seasons of weakness that we engage the world by the power of God's Spirit. Until we walk in that kind of power—until we embrace our own weakness—strongholds will stand in defiance against us.

Who is this coming up from the desert leaning on her lover?
(Song of Songs 8:5, NIV1984)

Satan leaped at the opportunity to tempt Jesus in His weakness. What Satan didn't understand was that Jesus was at His absolute strongest in the heat of the desert. In that place, the Father's strength carried Him, and Satan didn't really stand a chance. I can't help but wonder if that was God's plan all along.

When Satan exploited the limits of Jesus's human strength, Jesus leaned into the power of the Spirit. Satan could not have anticipated that Jesus (the "weak human") was created to walk in the power and glory of God. Even today, He fails to anticipate that God's power is strongest in our lives after we come to the end of our own strength.

> *But he said to me, 'My grace is sufficient for you, for my*
> *power is made perfect in weakness.' Therefore I will boast*
> *all the more gladly about my weaknesses, so that Christ's*
> *power may rest on me. (2 Corinthians 12:9)*

When God delivered Israel out of slavery in Egypt, in His sovereign authority, He led them into a very hot, very dry place. Out of the fire and into the frying pan. It was God's will that His people would wander the desert for a generation, so that they could learn how to follow His leadership, how to lean into Him for provision, and how to live as a people under covenant with the Lord. He meant this season to be a time when they would, inspired by His love for them, step into promise: priesthood, kingship, and sonship. He intended that they would discover their identity in Him. It was a time during which they would shed their slave mentality. He meant it for their weakness and, therefore, for an exponential increase of His power in them.

However much the people grumbled and complained about the heat, sand, and Moses's leadership—however much they rejected the identity God had spoken over them—they were never lost, forgotten, or abandoned by their God. In fact, the Angel of the Lord went before and behind them, and clouds of smoke and fire guided them by day and by night. God's message for Israel during this time must have been, "Just trust me, just follow me, and you will see."

Even after God's lavish displays of provision and love, the people of Israel grumbled through their desert, declaring to the heavens that they preferred their slavery back in Egypt to the pro-vided-for freedom they had in God.

The generation of freed slaves led by Moses never actually succeeded in renewing their enslaved minds. Tied to their slav-ery, Moses's generation missed its chance for deliverance into the Promised Land. As a result, the former slaves were buried in the sand of the desert, and the promise was passed to the next generation.

> *The rabble with them began to crave other food, and again the Israelites started wailing and said, 'If only we had meat to eat! We remember the fish we ate in Egypt at no cost— also the cucumbers, melons, leeks, onions and garlic. But now we have lost our appetite; we never see anything but this manna!' (Numbers 11:4-6)*

****

Israel's appetite for the "tasty" slave foods given to them in Egypt seems to have been one of the primary memories of slavery that held them back from promise. Unbelievably, they complained and grumbled to God because they wanted better food from Him. This happened! (It still happens. We do it all the time.) Esau made the same mistake in Genesis, when he traded his birthright to little brother Jacob for a bowl of soup. Adam and Eve did it when, ironi-cally, they were hungry to be like God. They ate the apple.

It is truly incredible, the things we will trade for our appetites. We exchange our destiny for some present gratification.

Israel, Esau, and Adam and Eve were hungry, but I would pro-pose they had no idea just how hungry they were.

> *As the deer pants for streams of water, so my soul pants for you, O God.*

My soul thirsts for God, for the living God.
When can I go and meet with God?
My tears have been my food day and night, while men say
to me all day long,
'Where is your God?' (Psalm 42:1-3, NIV1984)

There's nothing wrong with thirst, and there is nothing wrong with hunger—until we point them in the wrong direction.

Unfortunately, many of us haven't yet learned what David learned and pens in his forty-second song. If there is one thing we share as a generation, it is that we don't know how to quench our thirsts. We don't know how to manage our appetites. Like Israel, we have all sorts of urges, and we let them control and damage us.

David understood his appetite. He said, "My soul thirsts..." He understood that it wasn't just his body or his emotional life that were thirsty. David knew that there was nothing he could pump into his body or mind that would quench the thirst of his soul. He knew his hunger was much deeper than his flesh. He knew how to recognize his soul level thirst, and he knew that only God could quench it.

Here's what we tend to do: Our soul begins to thirst and we try to quench it with strictly physical or emotional things. Mostly, we turn to things that are very immediate, very tangible, and very temporary. We turn to relationships, entertainment, food, affirmation, media, sin, and others, and we expect our souls to drink deeply from these shallow wells. But our thirsty souls require a richer nourishment, they require water from God—water that's alive.

Drinking water from the wrong kind of source in order to meet our soul level thirst is like drinking water from a poisoned well. When you drink it, your thirst might get quenched, but you get sick. If you keep drinking it, you will probably die. We need to start drawing from the right wells for our nourishment—deep, clean wells.

Jesus is our righteousness. If we thirst for Him, we will be filled.

"Blessed are those who hunger and thirst for righteousness,
for they will be filled." (Matthew 5:6)

****

Israel never allowed its enslaved thinking to be freed by an encounter with the Father's love, so God held His nation in the desert. As a result, God chose to raise up a younger generation that would willingly step away from its heritage of slavery before it would walk into the Promised Land. The older generation died away, and the new emerged. With new leadership and new vision, and with the slave mentality removed a generation from them, God's young nation stepped into His love and walked into the Promised Land.

In the story of Israel's desert season, we see God's refusal to take slaves into His promises. He waits for a people who will rejoice and flourish in the freedom He has provided for them. He waits for a people willing to walk out of slavery and into sonship.

****

God didn't want a bunch of slaves abusing His land of milk and honey. This is fascinating. Some may look at God's refusal to allow mentally enslaved Israel into the Promised Land and think it a bit too harsh, but it really wasn't. God expects a lot out of His people. In requiring that they shed their enslaved-to-Egypt minds before He allowed them into the Promised Land, God proved Himself to be, once again, more glorious than we ever could have imagined.

His promised land is for His sons and daughters, not for a herd of ashamed ones wandering the desert. He wanted freed children who were willing to work and subdue His land, not entitled slaves who were useless without a slave driver. Slaves waiting on manna would have perished in the promise; God needed free children willing to work out and fight for His redemptive plan.

Don't be fooled into thinking that the title "son" is simply a lux-ury, though. Certainly, it is a luxury! But any father would expect more from his child than he would from a servant or slave. Any good father would believe in and value his child more than he would a hired hand. A good father would expect his child to live up to the father's opinion of what is possible for the child.

God raised the standard for His people in that moment. In not allowing a people who craved slavery to step into His promises, He revealed to us His requirement that we stand in Him, in dignity. In requiring His people to distance themselves from their slavery before they stepped into promise, He revealed His determination to let nothing short of sonship enter into destiny. He chose not to bless a self-imposed slavery, and He waited on them to realize that He expected them to own up to their value and worth to Him. Once they stepped into their actual identity, and once it was tested, He permit-ted them to step into the Promised Land.

This is a crucial connection to make: Identity and destiny go hand in hand. They have to. The identity we choose will place limits on the destiny into which we can step. Fortunately, we are free to choose an identity given to us by our Father, without limits, perhaps leading to a limitless, fantastic destiny.

In choosing to cede our identities to God, we allow ourselves to be blinded to our own opinions of what is possible. Most of the time, "blind" is bad, but this kind of blindness is very healthy. As believers, we need to walk through life blinded to our own finite (or wrong) fleshy expectations, limitations, and ideas of what is possible, so that they do not become barriers to our destinies. We need a vision that is bigger than ourselves. We need our own standard raised for us. If not, we set the bar far lower than God's standard of glory, and our fleshy destinies become merely shadows of the amazing plan God has for us.

That's what God did in the desert, when He made the "enslaved" generation stay in the desert places and invited His people of the next generation to come on in to the promise. God provides for us this incredible example of what is available in His Kingdom to those whose identities remain in Egypt and, in contrast, to those who receive the identity and inheritance He has for them as His beloved children. God-sized identity—God-sized destiny. Human-sized identity—human-sized destiny. It is a matter of identity.

In high school, I was one of the drum majors of my high school's marching band. (I was always much better at waving my arms around on tempo than I was at actually playing my trumpet. I also didn't like to march. So, I tried out to be drum major.) As drum majors go, I was nothing special, but I got the job done.

That was such a fun season of my life. We traveled across the state to go to marching band competitions, we won trophies, and we enjoyed being very good at what we did.

I was the leader of 140 high school students. As you might imagine, when you gather together any number of high school students—much less 140—stupid things happen. Some sort of herd instinct takes over when you put people together in large groups. What starts as a group of students can quickly turn into a crazy mess. Lots of fun, lots of chaos, lots of messes, lots of broken stuff everywhere, and lots of grumpy adult chaperones.

However, as the representative and drum major of the "best marching band" in the state of Arkansas, I didn't get to join in on the chaos. As the leader and baton-bearer of one of the strongest marching traditions around, I had to manage the chaos without contributing to it, a nearly impossible task. I carried the mantle, "leader." As the leader, I was held to a higher standard of behavior, honor, vision, and order than the rest of the band. The only thing that separated me from 140 of my peers was the drum major uniform I wore. My standards of behavior and dignity were raised the moment I received the identity, "drum major."

I still had a ton of fun, undoubtedly, and I enjoyed freedoms and privileges most of the other 140 never got to experience. I have plaques and trophies in my room at home that the 140 members weren't blessed to receive. Due to my duties and responsibilities, I had an awesome relationship with each of the band directors I worked alongside. I got my name in the newspaper. I had favor with people I didn't even know. I received scholarships. I wore a white jumpsuit, hat, and jacket combo that looked awesome. The only restriction: I couldn't act like an animal. I was called to set myself apart from the craziness that inevitably happens on a four-bus long caravan trip. I was told to be dignified, and I was expected to act as if I knew my value.

So it went for God's people in the desert. I received the title, "drum major," and my expectations, privileges, and destiny immediately changed. Israel received the title "sons and daughters," and their expectations, privileges, and destinies immediately changed. With the identity "child" came a raised standard, a greater responsibility, and a different destiny.

The identities we claim from God will determine the extent to which we walk in the land God has promised for us. God refused to grant His inheritance to "slaves," but He beckoned to those who knew they were sons.

Slave versus son. Wandering versus inheritance.

JESUS'S DESERT

Not only did God take His nation into a desert for refining, but He also led Himself into a desert, in Jesus.

As soon as Jesus was baptized, he went up out of the water. At that moment heaven was opened, and he saw the Spirit of God descending like a dove and lighting on him. And a voice from heaven said, 'This is my Son, Whom I love; with him I am well pleased.'

*Then Jesus was led by the Spirit into the desert to be
tempted by the devil. After fasting forty days and forty
nights, he was hungry. (Matthew 3:16-4:2)*

Immediately after Jesus was baptized, the Holy Spirit led Him directly into a desert. This passage says that the Holy Spirit led Jesus there to "be tempted by the devil." He was sent into the desert for testing. (Remember, God's Spirit will sometimes take us into uncomfortable places—including deserts. We need to come to terms with this.) He was sent into the desert, and His dependence on the Father was tested throughout His prayer and fasting.

We tend to think of desert seasons in a negative light, but like Israel's, Jesus's desert season was sent to Him directly from God. It was God's will and plan that Jesus would walk into that desert. It was the good kind of desert—the kind that is the will of the Father. Jesus, being perfect, would go on to provide a perfect example of how to handle a desert season—in utter dependence upon the Father and refusing to bow to the lies, shame, or chains of the enemy.

Jesus actually makes right Israel's foolish desert behavior. He manages His appetites, He stands in faith and dignity, and He obeys. Israel didn't know who they were, but Jesus certainly knew who He was. (*"You are my Son, whom I love..."*)

In the desert, Jesus's identity was tested. Refusing the religious spirit, He refused to "perform" for Satan. After proving His identity, He was released from the trying season.

In Jesus's desert season, Satan tempted Him. The interesting thing is that every lie Satan threw at Jesus was aimed at cushioning Jesus's desert experience. Satan actually tried to make the desert easier on Jesus; he tried to cut the season short. The temptations played to Jesus's human weaknesses and appetites. Read Matthew 4 and you will see that the first lie of Satan promised

Jesus a meal. The second lie would have resulted in Jesus's death or landed Him in the hands of angels. The third lie would have removed Jesus from under the authority of the Father and submitted Him to the authority of the Father of Lies. The lies of the Satan, in this instance of a God-ordained desert season, would have given Jesus an easy way out of His desert, but they would have violated Jesus's faith in the Father.

In addition to attacking Jesus's desert season, Satan attacked Jesus's identity. Each of the lies was introduced with doubt: "If you *really* are the Son of God..." Satan coupled his temptations with the insidious lie that the Father had not spoken the identity "Son" over Jesus. We should learn from this.

Temptation comes in conjunction with an attack on our identity, but if we anchor our identity to our sonship in Christ, the power of sin is truly canceled in our lives. The children of God who know they are considered royalty in the Father's Kingdom will inevitably see the manifestations of "It is finished" on the earth.

Satan attacks both our refining deserts and our sonship, because his desires for us are an identity in sin and a comfortable independence from the Father.

> *When the devil had finished all this tempting, he left him*
> *until an opportune time. Jesus returned to Galilee in the*
> *power of the Spirit, and news about him spread through the*
> *whole countryside. (Luke 4:13-14)*

This particular desert was clearly very important to God. This desert season was designed to prepare Jesus for His world-changing ministry. Some part of this season was deemed necessary by God to prepare Christ for the cross. He came up out of the desert "in the power of the Spirit." His victories over temptation in the desert prepared Jesus to walk into the Garden of Gethsemane victorious, regardless of the temptations to withdraw He undoubtedly faced leading up to His crucifixion. His weakness in His desert season was the foundation for His strength in drinking of the Father's wrath on our behalf. Leaning into the strength of the Father in His desert season, Jesus was clothed in power. It was in this desert that He was empowered by the Father to redeem everything.

When Jesus was clothed in the desert, His ministry became unstoppable.

****

It was in Jesus's personal breakthroughs and victories over Satan that He was equipped for global and corporate breakthrough and victory. Personal victory empowered Jesus to fight on behalf of His Church at the cross. Personal victory saw Him clothed in the power of the Spirit. In the verses immediately following the desert scene, Jesus begins His teaching and supernatural ministry.

The personal struggles you are going through, right now, are designed to make you powerful on someone else's behalf. The desert you are going through, right now, is designed to empower you to fight for breakthrough and victory in the Body of Christ. Your battles are making you stronger on behalf of the ones you are called to love. Slaves cannot break their own chains. That's where you come in, made powerful, as one who has gone before—just as Jesus went before us, made powerful, in His victories.

Proclamation of sonship -> desert testing -> clothed in power -> released into destiny. It happens in that order for a reason.

RETROSPECT

Deserts are never fun or easy, but that does not mean they are to be avoided. Deserts are good. Deserts, if they are from God, are *for* us and not *against* us. We walk out of desert seasons strengthened in supernatural ways. We leave deserts with a new dependence on God, and with a new knowledge of His faithfulness to us. We leave deserts confirmed in our identity in Christ.

We walk through deserts feeling alone, useless, and tempted. However, we leave them knowing that God was a pillar of fire before our eyes the entire way through, and that it was only ever His intent to prepare us to experience a new depth of His purpose for our lives. Deserts are good because God loves us.

In retrospect, my desert was good. My internal misery was very good because it was a pain founded upon broken idols. God brought me to my knees in this season, and He took away my idols so that I might worship Him. I am totally sold out to the fact that He broke me as gently and lovingly as was possible, and that He provided for me and led me in ways that I will never be able to understand. I know He rained manna on me when I was hungry, and I know He had His arms around me even when I believed the lie that I was alone. My desert was very good because God sent it my way. It made me so much better.

****

It's the broken bone principle. When you break a bone, it eventually heals. The cool thing is, the scar tissue of the bone is actually stronger than the original bone material. You break a bone and it heals back stronger than was at the start.

There are a lot of broken bones out there. I am one of them. The good news is that God is faithful to heal the bones He breaks. He is faithful to call us out of the deserts into which He leads us. He is faithful to bring rain to the places from which He has withdrawn rain. He is faithful to restore and bring to fullness. He is faithful to resurrect the faithful.

There is so much strength in broken bones. I am stronger for my broken season. I am a refined and redefined being. I'm a different person on this side of my desert. God used it to totally transform me. I couldn't possibly hope to explain how He did it, but He did it. He healed me—a broken bone.

I can testify through my story that there is redemption even in self-inflicted brokenness. God led me into a desert season, but shame crushed my bones while I was there. I looked a lot more like Israel than Jesus, while I was in my desert.

However, God is strong—far stronger than bones that break.

Right now, I know who I am.

****

Like Israel in their desert, I encountered the love, provision, and leading of the Father in my desert. He led me and He showed me aspects of Himself that I had never before experienced. Eventually, He called me to step into promised land with Him, but I foolishly clung to my memory of Egypt and my disgrace. Eventually, He called me into destiny, but I chose to stay a slave in the desert. With an unrenewed mind, and maintaining my refusal to believe that God *really* loved me as much as He said He did, I clung to the slavery and shame that had become my definition. I chose Satan's definition of my life (shame) over God's (son), just as Adam and Eve had.

I continued to cling to slavery until God gave me the faith required to step into who He says I am.

Understand, it is very difficult to part from what has come to *define* you. The people of Israel had a pillar of fire before them, and still they refused to believe that God was God, and that He loved them enough to lead them into the Promised Land. They saw God make a sea part for their safe passage, and still they clung to their memories of slavery in Egypt. They refused to believe He was who He said He was, and they refused to believe they were who He said they were. They refused to receive their new identities. They failed the test. They clung to their former definition.

In an absurd way, even in the midst of God's miracles and wonders, it is difficult for us to part from our former identities in order to claim the new identities given to us by God. Not only is it difficult; it takes death—Jesus's and ours.

This is what we need to understand today: Covered by the blood of Christ, and included in His death, it is our right as a people of liberty to step out of our identity of shame. Christ's death freed us and made us new. God will take us into deserts, or we will find ourselves in hot and dry places, but never are we bound there by our shame.

God will lead us into difficult places, according to His loving will, but He always calls us out in the power of His Spirit, if we prove faithful. If we are in a hot and dry place due to our shame, our sin, or Satan's lies, God offers us a way out, in Jesus. We can be free not only from Egypt, but also from a destiny choked out by a slave's shame.

God invites us to bury that enslaved part of us in the desert, and to move on into His promises. Bury the old you in the desert, just as Israel buried its older generation, and move on to claim the promises that God has for you. He has called us to come out of the wilderness in the power of His Spirit, leaning on Him.

> *The poor and needy search for water, but there is none;*
> *their tongues are parched with thirst.*
> *But I the Lord will answer them; I, the God of Israel, will*
> *not forsake them. I will make rivers flow on barren heights,*
> *and springs within the valleys.*
> *I will turn the desert into pools of water, and the parched*
> *ground into springs. I will put in the desert the cedar and*
> *the acacia, the myrtle and the olive.*

*I will set pines in the wasteland, the fir and
the cypress together,
So that people may see and know,
May consider and understand, that the hand of the Lord has
done this, that the Holy One of Israel has created it. (Isaiah
41:17-20, NIV1984)*

PRODIGAL SON, AGAIN

In his return to the father, the "lost son" was enchained by his slave mentality. He was his father's son, yet he sought only servanthood. He was setting himself up for a self-imposed desert season. However, the father's lavish display of love broke the slave mentality of his son. In joy and celebration, the father declared to his son an extreme kind of love. He declared grace and redemption, and he ignored the son's foolish desire to be only a slave in his father's house. With a tremendous sort of love, bigger than the limits and desires of the lost son, the father restored his son to sonship. He ignored the son's shame and foolishness, and he greeted him with a kiss.

The Father calls His children out of deserts with lavish displays of love. The lost son was convinced of his sonship when his father clothed him with his best robes, put a family ring back on his finger, and sacrificed the household's fattened calf in celebration of his return. The son was delivered from his shame by a revelation of his father's heart for him. He was restored to a place of power, authority, dignity, and identity in the father's house.

At the cross, God revealed His heart to us, just as the father revealed his heart to the lost son. The Father invites us to crucify our old, enslaved selves. He will wait until our enslaved identities are buried in the sand before He opens the way into promised things. His promises are for His children, for those willing to walk forward in His identity for them.

Therefore, if anyone is in Christ, he is a new creation; the old has gone, the new has come! All this is from God, who reconciled us to himself through Christ and gave us the ministry of reconciliation: that God was reconciling the world to himself in Christ, not counting men's sins against them. And he has committed to us the message of reconciliation. We are therefore Christ's ambassadors, as though God were making his appeal through us. We implore you on Christ's behalf: Be reconciled to God.
(2 Corinthians 5:17-20)

Part 2

Identity and Worth

CHAPTER 4

IMAGE BEARERS

This book is subtitled "Another Exodus" for a reason. Just as Israel had to make its famous exodus out of Egypt before it could enter the Promised Land, my generation of Christians must take our own exodus before we enter into the fullness of what God has for us. God has promises for us, just as He had for Israel.

He has somewhere for us to be. We should start moving in that direction.

In order to be authentically engaged with the world around us, we need to be fully alive. The world needs life. If we don't have life, we can't give it. The world needs joy. If we don't have joy, we can't give it. The world needs answers. If we don't have answers, we can't give them. It's the same with liberty. We can't give the world what we don't have, so we desperately need to step into spiritual freedom. Instead of running from the world, we should run into the world, a free people.

What does our Egypt look like? What do our chains look like? What does another exodus look like?

American Christianity's "chains" and "Egypt" exist in the form of our beliefs and the consequences of those beliefs. We are free to believe what we want (which is a very good thing), and we are free to believe what is wrong (which is also a very good thing). We exercise both of these freedoms, and we live through the consequences of both.

Our persecution and slavery is ideological and self-inflicted. The things we need to leave behind, the things holding us back from promise, exist in the form of lies. For Americans, and for many other people groups, false doctrine and false teaching are far more enslaving and damaging than political oppression or persecution. More often than experiencing persecution, we buy into incorrect "Christian" beliefs. More often than suffering abuse for what we believe, we are abused by what we believe. We buy into lies about who God is, what He thinks about us, and what He has called us into.

With our wrong beliefs comes slavery to something less than truth. This is the slavery that my generation needs to step out of: religion.

We have bought into a belief system from which we should run away. We need to reclaim truth for the sake of our freedom. "Another exodus" can come in many forms, but it will require that we reexamine what we believe. It will probably look like personal revival, and it will demand a greater knowledge of who Christ is. Intimacy with the Father and greater manifestations of the fruit of the Spirit will accompany our exodus. We will step into a greater knowledge of who we are, and thus be released into God's purpose for us to a greater degree.

****

At the beginning of this book, I mentioned that God's plan has never been our problem because it is perfect. God is incapable of falling short of His own standards because He *is* His perfect standards. In Scripture, God never holds back from displaying His glory. He is the God who puts the label "good" on everything He does. He is the God of excellence.

As humans, what are we? What happened with the arrival of sin and the chains that came with it? Are we not designed and implemented perfectly by our Father? As God's image bearers, are we *good* or are we *sinners*? What were we created to be? Where does the Fall of Humankind leave us? What are the ramifications of redemption?

In Christ, with God's Holy Spirit inside of us, what are we?

For we are God's workmanship, created in Christ Jesus to do good works, which God prepared in advance for us to do. (Ephesians 2:10, NIV1984)

For you created my inmost being; you knit me together in my mother's womb. I praise you because I am fearfully and wonderfully made; your works are wonderful, I know that full well. (Psalm 139:13-14)

EDEN

God set us in motion in Eden, so it makes sense to start there.

Then God said, 'Let us make man in our image, in our likeness, and let them rule over the fish of the sea and the birds of the air, over the livestock, over all the earth, and over all the creatures that move along the ground.'

So God created man in his own image,in the image of God he created him;male and female he created them.

God blessed them and said to them, 'Be fruitful and increase in number; fill the earth and subdue it. Rule over the fish of the sea and the birds of the air and over every living creature that moves on the ground.'

Then God said, 'I give you every seed-bearing plant on the face of the whole earth and every tree that has fruit with seed in it. They will be yours for food. And to all the beasts of the earth and all the birds of the air and all the creatures

> *that move on the ground—everything that has the breath*
> *of life in it—I give every green plant for food.' And it was so.*
>
> *God saw all that he had made, and it was very good. And*
> *there was evening, and there was morning—the sixth day.*
> *(Genesis 1:26-31)*

In this account of our creation, we get a glimpse into God's purpose for humankind. God placed tremendous value on us by creating us in His own image, complete with body, soul, and spirit. He gave us His own will, His own emotions, His own freedom, His own form, and His own creative potential.

After branding us with His image, by His mighty word He created the intended order for things: Humankind was to rule over all the earth and everything in it. In this passage, He charges humankind with the directive to rule this new and very good creation on His behalf. In short, He initially intended for us to be lords in His Kingdom.

His next command was to be fruitful and multiply, to fill the earth and subdue it. In this command, we see that it was His intention all along for Adam and Eve and their descendants to fill the earth, subduing it to establish the lordship and authority of the Kingdom. It was God's plan for His creation that humankind would actually partner with Him in exercizing God's authority within created order. For whatever reason, *we* were central to God's plan for creation. We were God's plan and strategy from the start. Sure, God could have done this without us. However, for reasons that are shrouded in mystery, He chose to spread the love and share this awesome task with His created children.

At the end of this passage, God judges His creation and determines that it is "very good." He looks at man, and at the world in which He placed him, and He is very pleased. In Adam, God sees an image of Himself, but with feet planted on the earth. At this initial judgment of the things He created, we find the foundation for our identity: God declares His image bearers to be part of something *very good.* He called us the *very good* lords of His *very good* creation.

According to God, our identity starts at "very good."

> *The Lord God formed the man from the dust of the ground and breathed into his nostrils the breath of life, and the man became a living being.*

> *Now the Lord God had planted a garden in the east, in Eden; and there he put the man he had formed. And the Lord God made all kinds of trees grow out of the ground— trees that were pleasing to the eye and good for food. In the middle of the garden were the tree of life and the tree of the knowledge of good and evil....*

> *The Lord God took the man and put him in the Garden of Eden to work it and take care of it. And the Lord God commanded the man, 'You are free to eat from any tree in the garden; but you must not eat from the tree of the knowledge of good and evil, for when you eat of it you will surely die.'*

> *The Lord God said, 'It is not good for the man to be alone. I will make a helper suitable for him.'....*

> *But for Adam no suitable helper was found. So the Lord God caused the man to fall into a deep sleep; and while he was sleeping, he took one of the man's ribs and closed up the place with flesh. Then the Lord God made a woman from the rib he had taken out of the man, and He brought her to the man.*

> *The man said, 'This is now bone of my bones and flesh of my flesh; she shall be called "woman," for she was taken out of man.'....*

The man and his wife were both naked, and
they felt no shame.

(Genesis 2:7-9, 15-18, 20-23, 25, NIV1984)

In this second creation account, we see Adam and Eve as the intended stewards and priests of the world God created. In this story, God makes man from the dust of the ground and breathes His Spirit into him, giving him life. He places His new image bearer in a garden paradise in the "east," near the tree of the knowledge of good and evil and the tree of life. The Lord places man in the Garden of Eden and gives him the directives to work it and take care of it.

If Eden was the Lord's first earthly temple, then Adam was its first priest. If Eden was the earth's first place of heavenly worship, then Adam and Eve were the first ones charged with the priestly duties to work and take care of God's house. If Eden was the first dwelling place for the Lord on earth, then Adam and Eve were most definitely called to be its priests. They would shepherd the place.

God provided His new creatures with trees that were pleasing to the eye and good for eating, but He forbade Adam from eating of the tree of the knowledge of good and evil. It is important to note that God never forbade Adam to partake of the tree of life. From what we are told in Genesis, the fruit of life was always freely available. It was death that was forbidden. Tragically, in our fall, we would choose death.

The only thing that God decided was "bad" in all of His creation was that Adam was alone. So He created for Adam his perfect match: Eve. The creation of Eve is a beautiful picture of the intimate relationship intended between husband and wife—Eve was literally *a part* of Adam.

It is interesting to see God's response to Adam's loneliness. Perhaps God saw His own perfect community within the Trinity (the Godhead), and He desired a similar fellowship for Adam. Perhaps He was thinking back to His "be fruitful and multiply" commandment and determined that Adam would not be very fruitful without a partner. We can't really know for certain why Adam without Eve was "not good," but we can take God at His word and know that the situation was, for some reason, not yet up to God's standards.

This second creation account in Genesis ends with the statement that the two—man and wife—were both naked in the garden, and that they were unashamed. They lived in a holy and obedient innocence before God, unaware of the knowledge of their nakedness. In Adam and Eve, all of huhumankind lived in holy and obedient innocence before God.

These two creation accounts clearly outline God's creative purpose for humankind. In the first account, God gives humankind authority to rule over His new creation on His behalf. He made us good lords of His good Kingdom. In the second account, God gives humankind the duty to tend to and take care of His earthly paradise. He made us in His image to be good priests and stewards of His earthly house, holy and blameless in His sight, naked and unashamed.

From the beginning of creation, humankind's identity has been charged with the duties of the kings and priests of God's heavenly Kingdom. We were made to be lords and priests for Him here on the earth.

According to God's design, we were *very good*.

NAKED AND ASHAMED

However, we fell. Something went very wrong:

> *Now the serpent was more crafty than any of the wild*
> *animals the Lord God had made. He said to the woman,*
> *'Did God really say, "You must not eat from any tree in the*
> *garden?"'*
>
> *The woman said to the serpent, 'We may eat fruit from the*
> *trees in the garden, but God did say, "You must not eat fruit*
> *from the tree that is in the middle of the garden, and you*
> *must not touch it, or you will die."'*
>
> *'You will not surely die,' the serpent said to the woman. 'For*
> *God knows that when you eat of it your eyes will be opened,*
> *and you will be like God, knowing good and evil.'*
>
> *When the woman saw that the fruit of the tree was good for*
> *food and pleasing to the eye, and also desirable for gaining*
> *wisdom, she took some and ate it. She also gave some to*
> *her husband, who was with her, and he ate it. Then the eyes*
> *of both of them were opened, and they realized they were*
> *naked; so they sewed fig leaves together and made cover-*
> *ings for themselves. (Genesis 3:1-7, NIV1984)*

The serpent was very crafty. He approached Eve with a lie, sneak-ily proposing to her that God told humankind not to eat of any of the trees in the garden. Eve innocently rose above the lie and cor-rected the serpent, explaining that they *were* invited to partake of any of the trees in the garden, except for the tree of the knowledge of good and evil. If the couple ate of the tree—if they even touched it—God had promised death for them.

After explaining God's rules and commandments to the ser-pent, Eve was outright deceived by him. The serpent told her that eating the fruit would actually make her like God. There was truth in what the serpent told her, but it was not the whole truth. Were they to eat the forbidden fruit, humankind's eyes would be opened, and they would indeed have been made like God in a *new* knowledge of good and evil. However, having been made in God's image, Adam and Eve were already meaningfully *like* God! The snake merely promised to them something they already had: access and likeness to the Father. One was merely according to the Father's will, and one was not.

The snake, with much irony, caused Eve to ignore the truth that she was made in God's image. He craftily placed God's wisdom and knowledge on a pedestal for her to see. The serpent lured Eve into idolizing the "fruit" of God, without regard to her friendship with God. He caused Eve to idolize only a fraction of God at the expense of the rest of God. The enemy's promises are dangerous.

Continuing on, the snake directly contradicted the Father when he spat the lie that death surely did not await Adam and Eve's ancestors, in their disobedience. Eve knew what the Father had said about dying, but the serpent countered God's word with his own deliberately false interpretation of the law. Using misdirection and lies, he enticed Eve with the assurance that she would gain great wisdom by partaking of the forbidden tree. The snake caused Eve to disregard consequences and covet rewards.

It is good that God withheld wisdom and knowledge from Adam and Eve. God knew that the tree of the knowledge of good and evil—the tree of religion, the tree of right and wrong, the tree of "achieving" righteousness, the tree of morality—would spell death for humankind. He even told us so! He knew that in our weakness, we couldn't handle the law and its fruit, which was represented by the tree of the knowledge of good and evil and its fruit. In forbidding its fruit, He was doing us a favor. He was forbidding death.

In love, though, He gave us open access to everything we needed for abundant life. In Genesis, He gave us the tree of life.

Further, He gave us free access to Himself, from whom all knowledge and wisdom flow. However, we were deceived into being dissatisfied. We had life, but we chose death. We had relationship, but we chose religion, law, and morality.

In his lies, the serpent never completely did away with truth. He bent it and proposed his own alternatives and additions. Relative "truth," subjectivity, and postmodernism were already present in the garden. The snake gave them options. He introduced seemingly good things that turned out to be very bad things. The snake introduced confusion.

Long story made short: Adam and Eve ate from the tree of the knowledge of good and evil.

Deceived and disobedient to the Father, Adam and Eve fell. They fell hard. You almost have to feel sorry for them, though. As responsible as they were for their disobedience to the Father (they knew *exactly* in whose image they were created and for whose glory they existed), we can feel sorry for them because they really were in over their heads.

While being tempted, Eve was innocent, for there is nothing evil about the ability to be tempted—even Jesus was tempted by Satan in the desert. Eve and Adam earned guilt, however, when they acted in obedience to the temptation. Humans became guilty when we willfully disobeyed God and gave our allegiance and obedience to sin and shame. We fell when we rejected God as our Lord and accepted Satan as His replacement.

We can pity Eve in that she really did not see it coming. The same holds true for us. Often, it is impossible to foresee the disastrous effects of the seemingly innocent things we do.

Satan made a very evil act of disobedience look like the innocent pursuit of a very good thing. He made what was actually disobedience to the Father look like good, pleasing, and desirable "wisdom." He made what was actually sin look like "likeness to

God," which must have seemed only a good thing to God's innocent children. Satan tricked Adam and Eve into disobediently pursuing God-likeness apart from submission to God, so they fell. He used Adam and Eve's hearts against them by convincing the two to go after *very good* things in a *very evil* way.

Are we not guilty of the same? All the time, we pursue good things apart from total submission to the Father's will.

When it comes down to it, Adam and Eve chose obedience to a lord that wasn't the Father, so God made them leave His garden paradise. Made aware of their nakedness, shame, and disobedience, they dropped out of moral perfection, and all of humankind since them has been stained and cursed by the effects of their (our) sin.

God had always called Adam and Eve "*very good*" lords and priests. Still, they chose allegiance and bondage to lies. They blew it all.

> In that day—'Sing about a fruitful vineyard: I, the Lord, watch over it; I water it continually. I guard it day and night so that no one may harm it.
>
> I am not angry.
>
> If only there were briers and thorns confronting me! I would march against them in battle; I would set them all on fine.
>
> Or else let them come to me for refuge; let them make peace with me, yes, let them make peace with me.' (Isaiah 27:2-5)

JEALOUS GOD

Imagine the wrath of the Father as He watched the effects of Satan's deception. Imagine His jealousy as His children told Him, by their actions, that His gifts, ordinances, and provisions simply were not enough. Imagine the pain in the pure heart of the Father as He watched His children disregard His trust and His Word. Imagine God's hatred for sin as He watched the fall of His beloved creation. Imagine what He must have felt when we rejected Him for a different lord.

Imagine what He must feel today when we choose different lords. We stumble over God's jealousy and God's wrath. However, from a good Father, wrath is due. His *very good* priests, kings, and children were warped from their created design by the effects of one lie. The ones He loves are walking in chains. His wrath is so due.

What we must realize is that His wrath against the sin in our lives and His jealousy for our affections reveal His desire for us. Moreover, I would argue that His wrath and jealousy reveal only the surface of His desire. I praise God that He is jealous for me. I praise God for His wrathful desire for me to walk in holiness and purity apart from sin. It means He wants me. It means He values me. It means that I am worth something to Him. It makes me valuable for all eternity. It means that, even in my sin, I matter enough to God that He would nail Himself to a tree to have me closer to Him.

So many of us know "God is love," but we find it hard to believe that God really wants us.

Sure, God hates sin because it is evil. But so much of the Father's hatred for sin is due to the damage it does to His children. He is fiercely and wrathfully in love with us. Wrath is poured out on sin because only our bondage and allegiance to sin stand between us and Him. He is jealous for us. He will fight for us. There is more to His love for us than the glory He receives from loving us perfectly. He actually loves, values, and delights in *us*.

*Lord, your hand is lifted high, but they do not see it. Let
them see your zeal for your people and be put to shame; let
the fire reserved for your enemies consume them.*
(Isaiah 26:11)

****

Maybe we don't understand the Bridegroom's jealousy for His
Bride because we live in an age when people give up on love.
Failed marriages, broken relationships, and all.

Maybe.

One of the most powerful promises in Scripture is the one
that guarantees our resurrected eternity with God will start with
a wedding feast. The Bridegroom—Jesus—will celebrate eternal
union with His Bride—the Church—in a heavenly wedding.

(Hope I'm invited...)

This one promise should cast an entirely new light on our relationship with God. He doesn't initiate eternity by inviting us into
His household as slaves, and He doesn't kick things off by hosting
a millennium long worship service. He begins our redeemed eternity by claiming us as Christ's Bride. At the outset of eternity, our
Lord marries us. He doesn't correct us, condemn us, or rebuke
us. After the Father presents His spotless Bride to Christ, we get
hitched. All of creation will witness this.

Jesus wants and loves us. If not, there would be no wedding.

When people believe that God's love for them abides by their
own poor, boring, and cold standards of love, they are bound to
miss out on most of what God has for them. But God's love is so
much greater than the world's fallen, secular "love." God's love
flows with marriage wine. Always. God's love is made concrete in

an unbreakable covenant. God's love is rich, intimate, pleasurable, and fun, and it never runs out.

Sometimes we fall into the trap of looking at our relationships with God only through the filters of our own worldly experiences. Jesus did not call us into the standard of love that this world holds; in fact, He shatters that standard and then raises the bar. Marriage was always meant to be loving, holy, and covenant because it was always meant to be an imitation and manifestation of Christ's love for His Bride. However, far too often, marriage is not those things, and lacks love, sacrifice, faithfulness, passion, and endurance. Covenant has given way to convenience.

Christ doesn't love His Bride according to our worldly standards of love and marriage. Christ calls our loving and our marriages up to His Heavenly standard.

Jesus doesn't love us with the kind of love that can give up. He doesn't conform to our 60 percent marriage success rate. He isn't a Bridegroom who is willing to let His marriage fail. He isn't cold, bored, or dissatisfied with us. Our Bridegroom's love for us is the kind of love that never fails. It's the kind of love that fights for the Bride: wrathful, passionate, jealous, sacrificial, faithful, and enduring. His is a love that will pursue our hearts forever.

But now, this is what the Lord says—he who created you, O Jacob, he who formed you, O Israel: 'Fear not, for I have redeemed you; I have summoned you by name; you are mine. (Isaiah 43:1, NIV1984)

No longer will they call you Deserted, or name your land Desolate. But you will be called Hephzibah ["my delight is in her"], and your land Beulah ["married"]; for the Lord will take delight in you, and your land will be married.

As a young man marries a maiden, so will your Builder marry you;

As a bridegroom rejoices over his bride, so will your God
rejoice over you.

(Isaiah 62:4-5, bracketed material mine)

BROKEN MIRRORS, BUT VERY GOOD

Before we fell, we were anything but "sinners." We were made in God's image. In Adam and Eve, we were *very good* kings and priests, holy and blameless before God. We were given authority to serve as lords over this creation, and we were made a priesthood that would care for God's earthly dwelling place. God would not have given such honor to a bunch of unholy things.

Before we fell, our default setting was not "sinner, " but *very good.* However, the reality is, we fell. We fell from perfection, and we stained God's image with our obedience to sin. Our fall explains our self-inflicted deserts, and it explains our chains and our shame.

When we fell, we became "sinners." We became a humanity in need of a savior. Yet before our fall, and even before He set the foundations of the earth in place, God set into motion His great redemptive plan. In His wisdom, God set into motion a plan of grace and love that would bring all of creation to its knees in worship. In His goodness, despite all the sin that He hated, He purposed all of His efforts in dealing with humanity toward one end: the restoration of humanity's *very goodness.*

Though God established covenant after covenant with His people, Israel, they remained a broken humanity that couldn't help but continue its cycle of falling. Throughout the history of His people, God remained perfectly faithful to His covenant, despite their disobedience. Even after lavish displays of love and provision, God's people would—with equal grandeur—turn their backs on their Father. Lavish betrayal has been in our blood since the Garden of Eden.

Still, God—in His goodness—remained committed to His plan to restore His creation to holiness and perfection. He did so because He is a faithful lover and friend.

Before we make Christ our Lord and Savior, we are this type of humanity. Before faith in Christ, we were fallen. We know this. We are intimately familiar with being the type of humanity that cannot help but betray God's love for us. Before the cross, we were the broken mirror images of God, with no hope. Until we reverse the decision made by Adam and Eve in the garden— the decision that rejected God's authority over man—we deserve our slavery to sin and Hell. Without Jesus's blood, we fall far short of God's standard for holiness and are, therefore, excluded from Him.

However, God's plan for humanity did not end at our fall. God's plan never ends short of redemption. He sent Jesus, and Jesus came to restore humankind. Jesus came to call us *very good* again.

In Christ, we are *very good.*

There is no room for crippling sin, shame, or bondage in God's definition of *very good.* The Holy Spirit tears those things from our lives as we step more and more into the revelation of who God says we are in Him: *very good.*

> *How great is the love the Father has lavished on us, that we should be called children of God! And that is what we are! The reason the world does not know us is that it did not know him. Dear friends, now we are children of God, and what we will be has not yet been made known.*
> *(1 John 3:1-2, NIV1984)*

> *On this mountain He will destroy the shroud that enfolds all peoples,*
>
> *the sheet that covers all nations; he will swallow up death forever.*

The Sovereign Lord will wipe away the tears from all faces;

he will remove the disgrace of his people from all the earth.

The Lord has spoken.

In that day they will say,

'Surely this is our God; we trusted in him, and he saved us.

This is the Lord, we trusted in him; let us rejoice
and be glad in his salvation.'

(Isaiah 25:7-9)

CHAPTER 5

RESTORED

God came as a man to restore humankind. Jesus's coming as a man approved who and what we are; when God became a human, He reaffirmed our design. He validated us. Certainly, God humbled Himself in becoming a man, but until He actually *became* our sins on the cross, our human form didn't blemish Him in any way. Jesus became a lowly servant, but there was no flaw in that. Though humbly low, He remained pristine. He calls believers to servanthood and humility, pointing to these as the hallmarks of His perfection.

Taking on flesh did not make Jesus dirty because there is nothing about God's untainted design—our *very good* humankind—that is dirty. Sinless Jesus was God's second approval of man's design. The first was in the Garden of Eden. In His perfect flesh, Jesus came to purchase us back from our enslavement to sin and death.

If there were anything flawed about a humankind absent of sin, God would not have told us that we were made in His image. If there were anything evil or unworthy about man's design, Jesus would not have come as a man. Our refusal to believe that is an insult to our maker and to the image in which we were made.

God's perfect plan for creation—our humanity—has never been our problem. Humanity's slavery to sin is the problem.

Let's get over the idea that *we* are the problem. We need to stop identifying with the *problem*. If we are in Christ, we are part of the *solution*. Once washed, there is nothing about us that makes us fundamentally evil creatures. If we are *evil*, even as the blood of Christ covers us, then the cross was a waste of God's time.

An inaccurate knowledge of our value and standing before God causes us to live inaccurate lives. If we do not believe we have been made worthy of God's love—if we believe we are *evil*—we will never fully enter into the potential we have to glorify Him. We will never enter into the promises that God has for us if we continue to define ourselves as His enemies.

We can't have the faith to see and walk in the amazing definition of God if we believe we are still defined by sin. It's impossible. Just as we must quit defining our relationships with God in terms of our sin, we need to quit defining our humanity in terms of our sin. Christ's blood removes us from our sin. We no longer need to identify with it. We can call ourselves worthless and evil all day long, but in Christ, God has called us *very good*. He has called us His sons and daughters.

Believers in Jesus Christ are no longer *sinners*. We are *redeemed*. The implications of this truth are huge. Our generation will find meaningful freedom in the truth of redemption.

****

There's a lot of wisdom in the idea of an "accountability partner," and accountability group meetings. As we address our weaknesses and build each other up, we are better for it.

That's great.

These meetings turn "ungreat," however, when intended to manage our sin. Knowing that you are obligated to confess your sin to your accountability partner every time you meet is a great disincentive to sin, right?

Ugh.

First, you can't manage your sin. Second, you don't have to.

So often, the only tangibles expressed by people talking "accountability" are the shame or humiliation experienced in exposing one's darkest areas to another person. We've systemized this shame and called it "accountability." We have welcomed a religious spirit, and we have placed it under the banner of "iron sharpening iron." It often leads to crushing disappointment and further shame.

People often give up and embrace their sin and shame. They realize that they can't fix themselves. They realize that "Christianity's" favorite answer to the problem of sin—accountability—can't fix it, either. So they consider themselves failures, hopeless sinners, or illegitimate believers. They see themselves as powerlessly distant from the grace of God, so they give up.

Don't get me wrong. There is absolutely nothing wrong with addressing your sins with a brother or sister Christian (in fact, this is biblical and necessary for healing), or with sharpening yourself in a small group setting. These things are very wise and they foster growth. However, the moment we decide that our peers and brothers are a means by which we get to freedom, we miss something. The moment we decide the answer to our sin is to simply create more rules and boundaries, we lose the battle. When we fool ourselves into believing that it's up to us to be sinless, it's a dead end road.

People can't free other people from sin. You can't free yourself from sin. That's God's job. We can only seek to become more like Jesus, desiring to see more of Him in us. We can only continue to surrender to Him. We can only ask Him for more grace to overcome more. We can only ask Him to heal us. We can only ask Him to consume our sinful desires with a burning desire to experience

Him more. We can make the decision to say no to sin, but it is Jesus in us and our fascination with Him that break the power of sin over our lives.

The purpose of accountability is to behold the Lamb of God. It is prayer, repentance, and the pursuit of healing. We become what we behold. Perhaps we are stuck in cycles of sin because we have traditionally beheld our sin. We meditate on our sin. We talk about our sin. We manage our sin. That's dangerous.

We become what we behold. Behold the Lamb.

(Sidenote: I have an accountability partner. I'm wiser and sharper for it, and I've found much healing through this relationship. However, I'm no cleaner. A good accountability partner speaks life, and will take you and your problems to the throne room, for the sake of healing. Your guilt, shame, and cleanliness are outside of the power of accountability.)

MADE WORTHY

Here is a pretty simple principle: Nothing deserves its worth. Worth is always determined by some external factor. Namely, worth is the price someone is willing to pay for something. If you are a believer in Jesus Christ, I'm about to tell you something that will fly in the face of every message you have ever heard that has ever called you anything short of *worthy*.

Get ready for it…

You are worthy.

Wham. There it was. Look out, here it is again: *You are worthy*.

As believers, we are worthy of God's love because He has called us so. We are infinitely valuable to God because He has called us so. We are important to God simply because He has called us so. Nothing we have done or ever could do makes us worthy of God's love. The fact of the matter is, God has called us worthy of His love.

We don't deserve our worth, just as we don't deserve His love, but He has transcended our fallen human opinions and has crowned us with both. Our worth is determined by the price someone is willing to pay for us.

We must ask the question, "How much (or what) did God pay for us that makes us so worthy?" The answer to that question is found back at the cross. Confronted with the problem of our infinite distance from Him, God purchased us back into His presence and priesthood with the blood of His very own Son. He didn't do this out of obligation. He loved us so much that He was willing to pay His Son's life in order to call us out of fallenness and into fullness.

At the cross, we see our *worth* to the Father.

We can dispose of the idea that God would waste His Son on a creation full of disgusting creatures that He had deemed unworthy. He didn't waste His Son; He *spent* His Son. He *spent* Jesus on the multitude of sons and daughters over which He rejoiced since *before* our moment of creation, regardless of the *sin* He must have seen coming. He *purchased* us. He *wants* us. He paid a *lot* for us. He *values* us. In God's eyes, our value and worth amount to *everything*. We were bought with the life and breath of His precious Son. God paid His *everything* for us, and I believe He would have paid more if He could have.

Christ's death declared to all creation that God values His children just as much as He values His very own life.

The cross was a statement of our worth to Him. It was a value statement.

SLAVE VS. SON

Toward the end of my time in depression, things were pretty terrible. I bottomed out in a hard way.

At my lowest, a sloppy mess, I sat on the floor of my room at home. Literally a sloppy mess—tears and snot everywhere. Anxiety, fear, uncertainty, and sorrow were all very present. I was convinced that I was alone, abandoned, and forsaken.

At the worst point, I bawled my eyes out, sprawled out on the floor of my room. I was crying out, but I wasn't crying out to God. I was just crying.

I really wanted to die. I can't explain how I felt in that moment. It was just absolute, infinite hopelessness. It was so dark that I wanted to end my life. This wasn't the first time I knew I wanted to die, but it was the only time I'd ever been certain I'd be better off dead. Before, I had always feared the unknown things of death, so I avoided it. This time, I knew death was preferable to what I was feeling. Suicide looked pretty good. So many lies.

Contemplating suicide is not a good place to be.

Still, there I was. Crying and alone, in a perfect storm of emotion, pain, and darkness. But then, something very strange happened.

"It's OK." God spoke to me.

At that time in my life, I didn't even know that such a thing could happen. Growing up in church, you hear stories of this happening, of course. However, you also hear stories like the one about a giant ark full of animals. (I mean, when's the last time you saw a giant ark full of animals?) The point is, this was totally unexpected.

"It's OK." At the edge of my life, God spoke to me...and He told me the truth.

At the time, I knew it was a supernatural thing because there was nothing OK about me in that moment. I wanted to be dead. The last thing I was feeling or thinking was, "It's OK." Nothing about me, my thoughts, or my situation was OK. However, as soon as I grabbed on to those two words that floated through my head, *peace descended on me. My pain and anxiety were calmed. I could think clearly. It was like a switch had been flipped. God shone a beam of light through the fog of my depression, and His peace settled on my heart and mind. It turned out, I wasn't alone in my solitary inner conflict.*

He spoke "OK" into being, and it saved my life.

It's funny how that one truth— It's OK"—brought an end to the thousands of lies I had bought into over a year's time. A multitude of lies whirred through my head, and one truth statement shot them all out of the air: one simple "It's OK" from the mouth of God.

In retrospect, the most amazing thing about that moment was that God was in the room with me. He was focused on me in my fit of tears and snot. He had honed in on me all along. He cares for, loves, and values me so much that He had His eyes on me even in my darkest, most shameful moment. I was worthy of His time that night, even in my shame. He valued me so much that He pulled me back from the brink of death, despite my mess. I lacked faith, joy, and dignity, but He was still for me.

I think many of us expect the exact opposite from God. We don't suspect that God wants to be around us in our dirtiness, so we work ourselves into hopeless "sloppy mess" situations like mine, totally shut down to the presence of God. We suspect that when we lack faith, God gets displeased with us. We suspect that when things are hard for us, God is embarrassed by us. We believe some pretty wrong things.

"It's OK." How many of us will be changed by this truth? How many need to know that God is actively involved in their worthy, yet painful little lives? We buy into a lot of lies concerning how miserable, disgusting, and unworthy we are, and these lead to even more lies and drain our hope even further. God would say to us in our distress, "It's OK." He'd have us know that things really are OK.

"It's OK."

Receive that if you need to, and let it change you.

****

What does this *worth* matter? It means everything, if we are concerned with living our lives from the place of knowing who we truly are in the eyes of God. With our faith in Christ's sacrifice, we are no longer disgusting, depraved, or disowned creatures. With Jesus's work finished, we can step into an incredible Father-child relationship with the creator of the universe.

God never stopped loving us when we became His enemies in our sin. In Jesus, we can step out of our bondage to evil and back into the affections that our Father has been pouring over us all along. At the cross, He takes away our bondage and filth and exposes us to the blood that forever makes us His children.

We need to come to an understanding of what the blood of Christ makes us. We have to live in a place of understanding our worth if we are to really glorify God.

"Sinner" versus "child." "Slave" versus "son." It really is a matter of choosing which name to live up to. We will grow into the name that we claim for ourselves. It is so easy for us to live up to the "sinner" label, but it's a much higher standard and calling to live as a child of God. By wrapping the chains of the title "sinner" around our lives, of course we will fall short and be disgusting, able only to walk in bondage and in the identity we have established for ourselves. If we step into truth, however, and acknowledge our God-given worth and identity, we can take off these limits!

When we choose between these identities, we establish boundary lines for our lives. We naturally grow to fill the boundaries.

We will never deserve to be called worthy, but in His grace, God calls us so, nonetheless. If we deny our worth, we reject God's opinion over our lives and choose instead to believe some lie that has taken truth's place.

God paid His Son for you. For such a price, God has named you *worthy*.

REDEEMED

This righteousness from God comes through faith in Jesus Christ to all who believe. There is no difference, for all have sinned and fall short of the glory of God, and are justified freely by his grace through the redemption that came by Christ Jesus. God presented him as a sacrifice of atonement, through faith in his blood...
(Romans 3:22-25, NIV1984)

In him we have redemption through his blood, the forgive-ness of sins, in accordance with the riches of God's grace that he lavished on us with all wisdom and understanding.
(Ephesians 1:7-8, NIV1984)

For he has rescued us from the dominion of darkness and brought us into the kingdom of the Son he loves, in whom we have redemption, the forgiveness of sins.
(Colossians 1:13-14, NIV1984)

SALVATION

The gift of redemption opens, pulling us into the Kingdom, when we place our faith in it. With the spilling of Christ's blood, *all* were given access to redemption—regardless of belief. Salvation comes with belief.

Lies keep so many from discovering the depths of their already completed freedom at the cross—believer and nonbeliever, alike.

If we only knew the ramifications of *"It is finished!"* Things would begin to look very supernatural.

Revelation of the truth of our redemption lifts the veil that blinds us to our freedom, already purchased. "It is finished." For salvation, we don't have to do anything but have a little faith that Jesus really wants us. He initiated and completed a love that we simply get to return.

When we think we are slaves, we behave like slaves. When we think we are damaged goods, we behave like damaged goods. However, when we believe we are loved, we are freed to behave as if we are loved. We get to step into sonship, and we get to act like sons. When we believe we are whole and made perfect, we are free to be whole and to rest in Christ's perfection.

Redemption, like the Fall of Humankind, is for *all*. God gave redemption to *all*. Salvation is for those who believe it. It is the measure of God's love for us, that He would redeem even His enemies, giving us the option to receive and return His love. God loves all, but we have to respond to it.

> *Accept one another, then, just as Christ accepted you, in order to bring praise to God. (Romans 15:7)*

When we accept truth, we are saved from lies. We are free to walk in relationship with Jesus.

****

I don't mean to minimize sin. Some will think that is my aim. I am not a Universalist, and I am not a Buddhist. I am not a New Ager. I think love wins always, but only when we let it win, through Christ. I think Hell is real. I think God's wrath is real, and I think some of my favorite people on this planet are going to spend their eternities very unhappy.

An eternity in God's Kingdom is only for those who unwrap their redemption in Christ, receive truth, and plug into the Kingdom of God.

God is beautiful, so sin is disgusting. Sin is a state of being and is the enemy of everything perfect and good. Because we are made in God's image, and because we are made more and more like Jesus by the power of God's Spirit, sin should disgust us. It should make us feel dirty. Slavery to sin should be extremely uncomfortable for us. In Christ, sin should feel absolutely unnatural.

We should rage against sin, as God does. We should make war against it, as God does. Sin should make our hearts sick, because that's what it does to the heart of our Father. We can better understand God's fiery jealousy for us in terms of the adulterous relationships we have with the sins in our lives. We provoke His jealousy by selling ourselves to lesser things. Sin provokes His wrath by seducing us.

In this book, I haven't intentionally minimized sin, but I suppose that sin has been minimized. Actually, I suppose that's to be expected. Our faith isn't about sin; it's about God. When we make God bigger, sin becomes smaller.

When we crucify our sin identities and take up our Christ identities, sin doesn't go away, but it is made powerless.

Jesus said to repent. He said to turn away from our sins. That's how Jesus addressed sin. He told us to walk away from it, turning instead to Him. I don't think He meant for us to keep peering over our shoulders, only to lock eyes with the sins behind us. To put words in Jesus's mouth: "Repent, quit beholding your sin, and come away with Me."

The thing is, if we tell people to stop sinning, they won't. Really, who do we think we are? Human strength and boundaries don't work when you're dealing with a lustful and persistent lover like sin.

However, if we give people a better, more faithful lover, they will eventually leave their sin behind. If we can help people to fall head over heels in love with Jesus, who is worthy, sin will be left in the dust as a byproduct. Hearts will be transformed, and outward purity and holiness will happen as peoples' love-wrecked hearts begin to spill over onto their dirty lives from the inside out. Freedom from sin just can't happen from the outside in. It is a matter of heart transformation.

It is a matter of giving ourselves just enough breathing room to fall more and more in love with the Lord. He takes care of the rest.

> The Lord is not slow in keeping his promise, as some understand slowness. He is patient with you, not wanting anyone to perish, but everyone to come to repentance. *(2 Peter 3:9)*

****

Repentance—turning away from the lordship of evil things—is necessary, and it is Christ's authority over death that gives us the power to do it. Jesus did not say, "Accept me into your heart." He said, "Repent, and follow me."

The only characteristic that separates those who will spend their eternity enjoying God from those who will spend their eternity suffering the wrath of God is the humility that leads to a repentant heart. Repentance leads a person away from the authority of sin and toward the authority of the Father. This repentant heart comes only with a revelation from God of the free love, grace, and mercy of the Father.

Belief in our redemption is freedom. In redemption is newness, cleansing, and healing. Chains fall away with the revelation that Christ—in His declaration of our redemption—chooses to ignore our shame. Like the prodigal son who was received by his father with joy, new robes, and a blood sacrifice, we are redeemed, purchased, forgiven, and made new. Redemption calls pitiful slaves into dignified sonship.

With faith in Christ's redemption, we are not defined by our sin. Our identity is no longer in our slavery to evil; it is in our newness in Christ.

> But now, this is what the Lord says—he who created you, O Jacob, he who formed you, O Israel:
>
> 'Fear not, for I have redeemed you; I have summoned you by name; you are mine.
>
> When you pass through the waters, I will be with you; and when you pass through the rivers, they will not sweep over you. When you walk through the fire, you will not be burned; the flames will not set you ablaze.
>
> For I am the Lord, your God, the Holy One of Israel, your Savior....
>
> Since you are precious and honored in my sight, and because I love you, I will give men in exchange for you, and people in exchange for your life. Do not be afraid, for I am with you...' (Isaiah 43:1-5, NIV1984)

A NEW IDENTITY

Reality? For the new creation in Christ, sin no longer has to be a part of the equation. We will sin in this life, but in Christ, the sin no longer defines us or our destiny. We are near to God. We no longer have to be subject to the guilt, condemnation, and shame that result from sin. We are "in Jesus." We are not rejected in sin; we are received in Christ.

Due to their slave mentalities, many believers in Christ refuse their freedom. This religious spirit is incoherent, schizophrenic, and foolish. It creates an identity crisis. Through faith in Christ, we are free. Our sin can be erased from our conversations. On this side of the blood of Christ, any sin we commit is a sin that we are free *not* to commit. We are no longer bound to obey sin. Christ gives us authority to say no to sin, and He frees us from the weighty consequences of sin. *Free.*

****

If you know me at all, you know that I really like cookies. If you don't know me, you now know one of the most important things about me. I really like cookies—to a fault.

When I see cookies, I have to eat them. They speak to me. They entice me. They convince me that they are worth it. At the mere sight of them, my mouth starts to water. I go out of my way to enjoy them. I dream about them. I mourn for them when the package is empty. I really, really like them. (It's bondage; if you were wondering.)

Recently though, I received a life-changing revelation from God. I am not kidding. I was walking through my church's lobby, making a beeline to the snack counter to grab a cookie, when God spoke to me regarding cookies. He even called me by name, which is hilarious and indicative of my condition.

As I reached for the cookie with a sense of shame, God's still, small voice said, "Bobby, you don't have to eat the cookie."

What do I think God was really saying? I think it was His way of saying, "Son, you are free. You have authority over this cookie. You can walk free from it."

I didn't have to eat the cookie. I have power over the cookie! Redeemed, I can say no to cookies! The cookies don't lord over me any longer. At the cross, the cookies were defeated, so I can walk outside of their unhealthy influence. Even though I don't really want to! I still desire cookies, but that doesn't mean I have to eat them.

So it is with sin. Freedom is yours, even if your flesh desires unhealthy slavery. A life of sanctification is just the process of your flesh (and its desires) catching up with the rest of you.

****

God saved us into a meaningful victory, through partnership with His Holy Spirit. We can call ourselves sinners all we want, but God does not. He does not want His children in bondage to that identity. He expects greater things. This is why He gave us His Holy Spirit. This is why Christ died to defeat death. This is why He calls us new creations. By the power of the Holy Spirit, we are free to walk through life separate from sin. Under His leadership and under submission to Him, we are called into victory over sin.

What empowers us is the knowledge that we do not have to fight for our victory over sin. In Christ, we stand on the battleground already victorious. In Christ's death, sin's authority over believers has already been defeated. This was a substantive victory; it means we can *actually* be free. He calls us into a standard of holiness in this life, and He sends us His Holy Spirit to help us make His standard our reality. He takes up residence inside of us to grant us the ability to live in that powerful freedom.

He gets much glory from our freedom. In Christ, I believe things begin to look a lot like Eden. By faith, and by the power of the Spirit, our lives are made to look *very good* again.

Then you will know the truth, and the truth will set you free....So if the Son sets you free, you will be free indeed. (John 8:32,36)

Our slavery—our sickness, our sin, and our shame—will end with the knowledge of just how deeply the Father longs for us to walk with Him through the trees in Eden, as Adam and Eve did. We are free from the chains of sin, because God's wrath at the cross has separated us from them. With faith in Christ's blood, we are reinstated to our created design: we are made priests and kings in the Kingdom of God.

On this side of the cross, we are *restored*. We are *very good*. This is our identity.

> *Forget the former things; do not dwell on the past. See, I am doing a new thing! Now it springs up; do you not perceive it? I am making a way in the desert and streams in the wasteland.*
>
> *The wild animals honor me, the jackals and the owls, because I provide water in the desert and streams in the wasteland, to give drink to my people, my chosen, the people I formed for myself that they may proclaim my praise.*
> *(Isaiah 43:18-21)*

LOVE SONG

The Gospel is a love song. It really is. Two thousand years ago, Jesus's coming was the flesh and blood rendition of King Solomon's, Song of Songs (or Song of Solomon). Solomon's ballad is the greatest love song ever written, and it prophetically spoke of King Jesus's love for His creation. Like the Song of Songs, the Gospel is the story of a God who is head over heels in love with His Bride. It is the story of pursuit, of love despite unfaithfulness, and of restoration. It is the story of healing, deliverance, and freedom.

Read the Song of Songs. It is an eight chapter picture of the love God has for His people. Solomon's song features a weak Bride who cannot help but fall short of the love of her Bridegroom. She is "dark, yet lovely." It also features a valiant and heroic Bridegroom who cannot help but be ravished by the love, however weak, of His Bride. He calls her perfect.

That's our story. The Song of Solomon is for us. It is the song that Jesus sings to His "dark, yet lovely" Church. We are His weak, made-for-Him Bride.

In terms of our relationship and restoration, the Song of Solomon sums up our marriage to Christ better than I ever could.

Who is this coming up from the desert leaning on her lover?
(Song of Solomon 8:5, NIV1984)

Christ is such a faithful lover. He is faithful to let His broken Bride lean upon Him, made perfect in our nearness to Him. We wander off into deserts—sometimes led by the Spirit—and Christ is faithful to retrieve us. Even dirtied and broken, leaning on Him is OK. The dark, lost, and dirty Bride seen coming out of the desert is the same Bride that He calls His "beloved." It is the perfected beloved of many trials. God calls His beloved to lean into Him, and a mature beloved *will* lean. He wants to marry this weak Bride. He wants to marry us.

He calls us to Him, even in our weakness. He calls us into tender, intimate relationship, despite our shortcomings. In our weakness, His love and joy are our strength. Apart from Him, who have we really to lean on? It is in this place of willing dependence on Him that Christ makes us new again. We are restored when we lean, when we let ourselves be humbly weak. We walk rightly with Him only when we are leaning into Him.

CHAPTER 6

JARS OF CLAY

We were created to be *very good* in God's image. We were made to be kings and priests in God's heavenly Kingdom, and all was well with the world before we derailed God's created plan for us. We fell, became covered in sin, earned guilt and judgment, and became disgraceful things. We were made dirty by our disobedience to God.

However, that is not the end of the story—praise God!

Jesus came and redeemed us. The Father sacrificed His Son, and we are saved because of it, by faith. He paid everything to tear our sins away from us. In Christ, we are no longer slaves, but sons. We are no longer sinners, but *very good.* We are made new. We are made kings and priests, and we are given authority over the sin that Christ defeated on our behalf.

This is all very good news. However, just as it was with our fall, it is not the end of the story.

As of yet, I have made redeemed humanity sound very awesome. And we are awesome! God's work of redemption in our lives is a very good, supernatural, and miraculous thing. *We* are very good, supernatural, and miraculous things. God has made us into beautiful, incredible things. Sin has no authority over us.

Redeemed humanity is kind of a big deal. However, we are still people, and God is still God.

In our freedom from sin, and in our authority over darkness, there are new dangers. Cut loose from our sin and its consequences, many have the tendency to forget that, redeemed from sin, we are still completely and utterly dependent upon God. With the revelation that our sins (for many, the focal point of their relationship with God) are forever washed away, some will be left wondering how to interact with God. After our redemption, all begging, shame, and false humility before the Father flies out the window. Now what?

The whole point of stressing that the Gospel is built on the heart of the Father, and not on our own sin, is that it does not make sense that our relationships with God hinge upon our sin. Our sin did not create our relationship with, love for, or dependence upon the Father. It created our distance from Him and our need for mercy. Even on this side of redemption, with sins removed, it continues to be in our design to depend on the Father. Free from sin, our need for Him is still absolute.

With our need for redemption satisfied, it can be easy for us to fail in acknowledging our present *need* for God. In our freedom, we can fail to recognize *why* we are free: To worship and bring glory to the Father, leaning into His power to get the job done. With our shame removed, we struggle to find humility. We get comfortable and, eventually, prideful. Made clean in our intimacy with the Almighty, we forget to see our weakness.

Washed by the blood of Christ, we are still called to submission and humility before the Father. A humanity set free will always depend on Him. Praise God—we need Him.

****

It blows my mind to realize that Jesus Christ trusts me. He definitely should not trust me, and He knows it. Still, He trusts me, anyway. He trusts me, probably because He knows my identity better than I ever will. He chooses to see me as a priest and king of His Kingdom. He chooses not to remember my shame.

Not only does He trust me, but also He relies on me. He counts on me. He has called me to partner with Him in His ministry of reconciliation. This is mind-blowing.

Why shouldn't He trust me? Because I'm a traitor.

Aren't we all? Don't we, on a daily basis, fail to live up to the glory of God? Don't we even fail, on a daily basis, to live up to our own glory, which was given to us in Christ? Don't we prove to be unfaithful lovers each time we give ourselves into the hands of adulterous sin? Isn't each failure simply another nail in His flesh?

The ground level reality is, we are weak. We mess up. We fail to walk in the strength of God, so we fall to sin.

God loved Judas, even with the knowledge that Judas planned to betray Jesus. In fact, Jesus walked with Judas for nearly two and a half years, perhaps with this knowledge. Still, Jesus loved him. He still died for him. Until the very end, He still called him a friend.

I know Jesus's love for me. Sometimes, very aware of my weakness, I find myself reminding Jesus that I can't really be trusted. I let Him know that I won't hold it against Him if He reconsiders trusting me because I didn't deserve it in the first place. I'm a lot like Judas.

"Surely, Jesus, You know that I will betray You!" I say, but He ignores me.

He ignores our foolishness and chooses instead to delight in us. He delights in our hearts, despite our shame, because He sees our identity in Him. He sees that we have committed ourselves to Him, however weak that commitment may be. He sees that we understand, deep down, that we are nothing apart from Him, and He sees a people with whom He can work. He sees that we desire to make Him happy, and He receives that as love.

Jesus delights in us, even in our weak attempts. He definitely delights in our extravagant successes. However, I think He delights in all the silly hearts set on not letting Him down.

We love Him with our weak hearts, and He loves our weakness, powerfully.

WEAKNESS

I think we all go through life for days, weeks, or months at a time, operating under our own strength and ability, experiencing life from a position of brittle invulnerability. We climb to the top of our little world and wrestle everything into submission. We go through life conforming to a culture that says, "Anything less than power, authority, and perfection is weakness, and weakness is bad, pitiful, and sad." Walking successfully in our own power, we begin to think that we, in addition to being *very good,* are *very strong.* We eat up this lie, pushing ourselves to greater levels of false security and false strength.

Then, all of the sudden...WHAM! God reminds us that we aren't Him, and we come to realize our weakness.

> *For God, who said, 'Let light shine out of darkness,' made his light shine in our hearts to give us the light of the knowledge of the glory of God in the face of Christ. But we have this treasure in jars of clay to show that this all-surpassing power is from God and not from us.*
>
> *We are hard pressed on every side, but not crushed; perplexed, but not in despair; persecuted, but not abandoned; struck down, but not destroyed. We always carry around in our body the death of Jesus, so that the life of Jesus may also be revealed in our body. (2 Corinthians 4:6-10, NIV1984)*

The truth is, our human weakness is part of God's plan. It is God-glorifying. In fact, God went so far as to look upon Adam's limited and finite frame—upon Adam's human *weakness*—and He called it *very good*.

It is important to define "weakness." I am not talking about moral imperfection. Evil is not God-glorifying, and it certainly is not "very good." When I say we are weak, and that our weakness is part of God's plan, I mean only the obvious: Humans are much less than God, and we were created to depend on Him. We are weak because *we*, unlike *God*, have limited strength, energy, endurance, capabilities, capacities, talent, power, love, will, grace, forgiveness, faithfulness, ability to withstand temptation, and more. We are weak, so we are susceptible to falling.

God is God, and we are not. (Maybe this is what God meant when He said, "I AM.")

In his letter to the Corinthian church, Paul calls us "jars of clay." Undoubtedly, we are beautifully and perfectly designed "jars." We have in our design an intricacy that speaks volumes of God's majesty. The thing is, while we jars are indeed wonderfully and perfectly made, we are made out of *clay*. We are glorified dirt (literally). There is nothing particularly wonderful about dirt. And things that are made out of *clay* will always be fragile.

In the grand scheme of God, *clay jars* are very weak. Compared with the heavenly beings we see in Scripture, we—God's image—are *weak*. In light of the stars and galaxies flying past each other through outer space, we—the center of God's affection—are pretty *weak*. Humans, in and of ourselves, are not strong.

Why did God make us breakable, fragile, and dependent? Why is it okay ("very good," according to God) that we are created to be limited? Why does our weakness bring God glory?

> *A voice says, 'Cry out.'*
>
> *And I said, 'What shall I cry?'*
>
> *'All men are like grass, and all their glory is like the flowers of the field. The grass withers and the flowers fall, because the breath of the Lord blows on them. Surely the people are grass. The grass withers and the flowers fall, but the word of our God stands forever.'*
>
> *(Isaiah 40:6-8, NIV1984)*

LESS OF ME, MORE OF HIM

God made us "jars of clay" so that He could put something *in* us. He made us dependent, so that we would be set up for success in our dependence upon Him. Truly, we should *desire* and *love* fellowship with God, but how easy would it be for us to remain distant from Him if we could get away with not *needing* Him? It would be far too tempting for us to be our own God, if we could actually function as our own God. Fortunately, we cannot. We cannot stand under that kind of pressure.

Remember:

> *For God, who said, 'Let light shine out of darkness,' made his light shine in our hearts to give us the light of the knowledge of the glory of God in the face of Christ. But we have this treasure in jars of clay to show that this all-surpassing power is from God and not from us.*
> *(2 Corinthians 4:6-7, NIV1984)*

There is a bizarre tension in the truth of our human weakness. As flesh and bone (our form) we are limited and weak, but as children of God (our definition) we bear a vast treasure and are called to power. We have to reconcile our human weakness to the fact that, as God's servants and children, we are "more than conquerors." Even in our fragility, God calls us to arms—to fight spiritual battles, to don armor, to heal, to loose chains, to cast out evil, and to pierce darkness with a light that He has made ours.

The question is, how do we reconcile those two truths? How can we be weak clay jars and yet walk in victory as kings and priests on the earth?

To be victorious clay jars, we must truly humble ourselves, acknowledge our clay form, and choose to lean into the power and provision that God has promised for His children. Knowing we are only clay vessels, it follows that without Him, we could do the incredible things God calls us to do. Clay jars can't conquer anything. As limited and finite clay, we have no real claims to strength.

In order for our weaknesses to mesh with our calling to walk through life in authority over darkness, we have to live up to our side of God's promises for us. We have to know and celebrate that we need God and that we cannot do (and should not attempt to do) God-sized things without God. We have to embrace our "jarry" humility and weakness, and we must take it by faith that God will make good on His promises when we lean into Him. When we do this, God faithfully lives up to His end of the deal by filling us jars of clay with His treasure. When we stand on His promises, believe on His faithfulness, and approach Him in our humble need, He substitutes His strength for our weakness. When we lower ourselves before Him, He fights our battles for us.

In order to find strength in our clay weakness, we have to find our humility.

Covered by the blood of Christ, any power or authority we have over darkness—over sin, over Satan—will be given to us by the Father. We have no strength apart from Him.

In our weakness, God does the heavy lifting. He wants to fight for us, He wants to show off for us, and He wants to show His faithfulness to us.

What good father doesn't do these things for his children? What good father doesn't desire to fight for his kids? What good father doesn't want to impress his household? Our Father wants us to depend on Him, and He wants us to adore Him. Sometimes, He is more "daddy" than "Lord."

Further, God calls us to do tremendous things for His Kingdom, regardless of our own weaknesses, to make His power known. There is no mistaking God's power, authority, and sovereignty when a *clay jar* moves a *mountain*. One of God's favorite ways of attracting attention to Himself has got to be by using weak, breakable, and seemingly ineffectual clay jars to fight and win wars for His Kingdom. The Father's glory cannot be ignored when one of His redeemed children—weak in its clay form—is empowered by the Holy Spirit to bring liberty, light, and living water into dying places.

In our dependence on Him, He is greatly glorified.

God knows the truth that clay jars cannot, on their own, produce God-sized results. He knows this truth, and He uses it to put His glory on display. God is greatly glorified, and we are greatly empowered when we allow *His* treasure to spill out of *our* clay jar.

*Do you not know that your body is a temple of the Holy
Spirit, who is in you, whom you have received from God?
You are not your own; you were bought at a price...*
(1 Corinthians 6:19-20, NIV1984)

HUMILITY

One thing we are very good at is false humility. We have this perception that what keeps us humble is our sin, but this is a lie. Our humility must not be founded on our *sin*; it must be founded on *God*. Our humility can reference our weakness, but it should never depend on our sin.

Sin does not make us humble; it makes us dirty. It disgraces us. When the Father called us to be humble, and poor in spirit, He was not calling us to think poorly of ourselves. Why would He call us *very good* in Christ, and then demand that we refuse to think of ourselves in those terms? Why would He make us perfect in His sight, and then demand that we call ourselves dirty and lowly? He wouldn't wash our sins away, while expecting us to stew in the memory of them.

Our call to humility before God is a call to acknowledge that He is infinitely greater than all things. Our call to humility before others is a call to make and treat others as greatly valuable to us. Simply put, He calls us to treat Him and others as valuable and worthy, before we treat ourselves as such. Humility is a counter to pride, and it has nothing to do with our sin. It is a thing of perspective and honor.

As we let God be who He is, infinite God, we can start to think more highly of ourselves in relationship to Him. As we ascribe more value to others, we can start to think more highly of ourselves in relationship to them. Small, tarnished views of God and people require a small, tarnished view of ourselves, if we are to remain "humble." However, if we put things into perspective—if we honor God and those around us—we gain a permission we had previously forfeited, to think of ourselves with dignity. We gain a permission to know that we are important and valuable, while still retaining our humility before the Father and others.

When it comes down to it, a "humility" based on sin is really just disgrace. A "humility" founded on sin is just shame, disappointment, or disgust. It's a lowering of our own value, contrary to what God thinks about us, because of some way that we have fallen short. Guilt, condemnation, worthlessness are not meant to belong in humble hearts.

We need a redefinition of humility. We need to found our poorness in spirit on the greatness, power, and perfection of our God, and not on our moral failures.

A right knowledge of our weakness will contribute greatly to our humility. However, it is critical to remember that our weakness is a very different thing from our sin. The Father pours out wrath over sin, but He delights over our human weakness. He delights in our dependence on Him. Sin deserves God's wrath, but He calls our weakness *very good.*

Our humility, just like the rest of our faith, needs to be centered on God and not on sin. The Father is great and mighty, we need Him, and we can contribute nothing to Him (except joy); therefore, we are humble. Covered in Christ's blood, sin need not be in the equation of humility.

IN CHRIST

The most important thing about our identity is the strength we have in Christ. As humans, we *are* weak. What really defines us is our dependence upon God. It is our humility and our childhood under the Father that includes us in the equation of His redemptive plan for all things.

> *My prayer is not for them alone. I pray also for those who*
> *will believe in me through their message, that all of them*
> *may be one, Father, just as you are in me and I am in you.*
> *May they also be in us so that the world may believe that*
> *you have sent me. I have given them the glory that you*
> *gave me, that they may be one as we are one: I in them and*
> *you in me. May they be brought to complete unity to let the*
> *world know that you sent me and have loved them even*
> *as you have loved me.*
> *(John 17:20-23, NIV1984)*

When we profess faith in Christ, we actually become in Christ. Some of the grandest promises to which we have access in Scripture have to do with our inclusion in Christ. It is a supernatural and mysterious thing, but when the Father looks on an imperfect person covered by the blood of His Son, He sees His perfect Son. A person with faith in Jesus becomes one with Jesus, and the Father makes no distinction. He has no favorites. The same love that He pours out on Jesus, He pours out on those who are in Christ. When we put our faith in Christ, we are pulled into Christ's sonship.

When we choose to identify with Christ, the Father identifies us with Christ. We become co-heirs and co-conquerors with Christ. We follow in Christ's footsteps, we are made like Christ, and we are promoted to His standards of perfection and holiness. We are crucified in Christ, resurrected in Christ, and seated at the right hand of the Father, in Christ. We are seated with Christ in heavenly places. Christ's promises are our promises. He commissions us to partake in His ministry. Humbly submitted to this, He gives us the authority He receives from the Father. Redeemed, we are in Christ. This is God's grace in action.

All of these things are *very real.* "In Christ" is not some abstract. "In Christ" is the realest, most amazing thing about us. It's who we are.

I am the vine; you are the branches. If a man remains in me and I in him, he will bear much fruit; apart from me you can do nothing. (John 15:5, NIV1984)

But he who unites himself with the Lord is one with him in spirit. (1 Corinthians 6:17, NIV1984)

Now you are the body of Christ, and each one of you is a part of it. (1 Corinthians 12:27)

*For in Christ all the fullness of the Deity lives in bodily form,
and you have been given fullness in Christ, who is the head
over every power and authority.
(Colossians 2:9-10, NIV1984)*

*For you died, and your life is now hidden with Christ in God.
When Christ, who is your life, appears, then you also will
appear with him in glory. (Colossians 3:3-4)*

*God made him who had no sin to be sin for us, so that in him
we might become the righteousness of God.
(2 Corinthians 5:21)*

*And God raised us up with Christ and seated us with him
in the heavenly realms in Christ Jesus, in order that in the
coming ages he might show the incomparable riches of his
grace, expressed in his kindness to us in Christ Jesus.
(Ephesians 2:6-7)*

*In him and through faith in him we may approach God with
freedom and confidence. (Ephesians 3:12)*

CHRIST IN US

If all that were not enough, Christ is *in* us. According to Colossians, the fullness of the mystery of God is revealed to us in the miracle of "Christ in us." God's grand plan for humankind—the sum of His work for our redemption—can be found in Christ in us:

*I have become its servant by the commission God gave me
to present to you the word of God in its fullness—the mystery that has been kept hidden for ages and generations,
but is now disclosed to the saints. To them God has chosen
to make known among the Gentiles the glorious riches*

of this mystery, which is Christ in you, the hope of glory.
(Colossians 1:25-27, NIV1984)

Christ in us is the vast treasure that God places inside His very weak and seemingly ineffectual clay jars. Christ in us is the person of the Holy Spirit, who has made our bodies His dwelling place. It is God in us, for the purpose of equipping us to do God's work. It is our hope of glory. It is our strength and power.

God is not a fool. He is aware of our human weaknesses. He is aware that there is a very real enemy, Satan, who apparently is also very aware of our human weaknesses. God knows our Edenic naïveté and our tendency to believe Satan's lies. However *very good* He says we are, God knows we are still just clay jars. He knows we can't live up to His calling without His help. He knows we need Him.

Acutely aware of our hopelessness without Him, He takes up residence within us to meet us at our created need. He dwells in us to help us in advancing His agenda. He is the great enabler of the kings and priests of His very own Kingdom. God's Holy Spirit in us empowers us to bring Him glory by providing for us our strength. He reveals to us the very God whose glory we are to declare to all creation. God's Holy Spirit dwelling within us, never leaving or forsaking us, is Christ in us.

Christ in us should blow our minds. That we have the Holy Spirit of God inside of us, at this very moment, should shatter all the limits we have placed on our lives. That *God* is currently within our beings, in His entirety, should change the way we think about ourselves and the world around us.

"Christ in us" means that the *fullness* of God lives inside of us. It means our words have creative power. It means we have the ability to bring life to people, and it means we can shine for His glory, by His power. It means there is no barrier between God and us because He has erased the distance between us. He leaped into our bodies, bringing His Kingdom with Him.

> *For through him we both have access to the Father by one Spirit. (Ephesians 2:18)*

> *Now it is God who makes both us and you stand firm in Christ. He anointed us, set his seal of ownership on us, and put his Spirit in our hearts as a deposit, guaranteeing what is to come. (2 Corinthians 21-22)*

Furthermore, in Paul's first letter to the Corinthian church, he reveals that the Holy Spirit searches the depths of the mind of God, and that the Spirit reveals things to those who are led by Him. Put simply, the Spirit searches the depths of God's wisdom and knowledge, and He reveals to us what He finds. This means that with Christ in us, we have access to the mind of Christ. With God in us, we have access to His will, His thoughts, and His emotions, as the Holy Spirit sees fit to reveal them to us.

God is in us; He is closer to us than anything else. The wall keeping us distant from God is a lie. His Spirit is *in* us, regardless of how dirty we think we are. He is closer to us than our bones. With Him in us, we have access to blanket authority over the kingdom of darkness, which Christ defeated at the cross. With faith, we have the ability to move mountains and walk in miracles. We clay jars house the God of the universe, and this was His plan for our redemption from the start.

"Christ in us" is kind of a big deal. It makes us very supernatural beings. It makes us walking miracles. On our own, we are so *weak*. However, with God in our being, we become miraculously *able*. In Christ, we are capable of bringing all sorts of glory to the Father, because in Christ, we are *strong*. In our *weakness*, Christ is strong in us.

FREEDOM

This is very good news for a generation in chains. The Spirit of God is inside of us, and where the Spirit of the Lord is, there is liberty. According to these realities, we are free. With God in us, our slavery to sin, shame, evil (and all its consequences) are nothing more than a realistic fiction. They are lies that we can say no to, however often we experience them. Freedom, for our generation, is as simple as stepping out of our deserts and chains, by the power of the God that is in us, and into the alternative reference point of Kingdom liberty.

Therefore, there is now no condemnation for those who are in Christ Jesus, because through Christ Jesus the law of the Spirit who gives life has set you free from the law of sin and death. (Romans 8:1-2)

We can call ourselves sinners, but on this side of the cross, our Father calls us much greater things. We have the mind of Christ, we are in Christ, and Christ is in us— surely, we are more than sinners. We are His sons, kings, and priests, and He calls us *very good,* righteous, and made perfect. The name "sinner" falls short of those things. We are free from that depraved title.

We are still people, and God is still God, but in Christ, we are made far more significant than (perhaps) we can understand.

The spirit of sin-centered religion in my generation will shudder at the thought that we are *very good.* The religious spirit will cause many to shrink back from the reality that God has called us *worthy.* It will cause some to run away from the implications of being *in Christ.* We are so used to being told that we are cheap, disgusting, unworthy, fallen, depraved, and more, that many of us will find it difficult to see the marvelous truth of how *worthy* we are according to God. Many of us will think that stepping into these grand descriptions is prideful. Others will think that calling ourselves *very good* is just another attempt to make a very sad generation feel better about itself.

The reality is that God calls us all those amazing things. God leaped across the distance between Him and us, in pursuit of our hearts, to fill our lives with His presence. God determined that we are worth the blood of His Son to Him. God first loved us so that we might love Him, and He gives us the very faith by which to do it. God is fiercely in love with His spotless Bride.

By the blood of Christ we are *very good* beings because God says so. Yes, in light of our sin and shame, all of this is too good to be true, but this is the whole point of grace. We do not deserve these grand identities, and we never will. However, we simply cannot afford to disregard what God has spoken over us because we believe we do not deserve it. When we do that, we begin to waste our lives.

He has chosen to use us as His strategy for being glorified in creation. For that glory to come, God needs a multitude of slaves to step into sonship and into freedom. He needs His people to receive His love. He needs us to dance out of our fallen realities and into His arms.

So much of the chains, bondage, and drought in my generation are due to a lack of the knowledge of who God says we are. So much of our shame and pain are due to a failure to understand what it means that God loves us perfectly. It wasn't enough for Him that He died for us. To get His point across, He put Himself in us to free us. Nearness and intimacy were not enough; unity was the end goal.

He is calling us out of our deserts, and He has already done all the work for us. He is calling us out of slavery and shame and into a completed and sufficient freedom. At the cross, He beckons us into His Kingdom, for His glory. If we are still walking as slaves, we merely do not understand how loved we really are.

****

There is so much hope for our generation. Even if you are walking through a desert at this moment, there is so much hope.

In Old Testament times, a good shepherd would break the leg of a sheep if it wandered away from the flock. This was the standard 2,000 years ago, and it is the standard today. Breaking the sheep's leg might seem brutal, but we have to understand that the shepherd knew things that neither the sheep nor we understand. In the interest of saving a sheep from some unseen disaster down the road the next time it wandered away—to save it from its own foolishness—the shepherd breaks the silly animal's leg. (Better its leg than its neck.)

This served at least two purposes: First, it let the sheep know that it shouldn't have wandered away from the flock. Second, it temporarily immobilized the sheep, preventing it from immediately wandering away from the flock a second time. This approach was very effective.

The best part about it was that the sheep couldn't walk with its broken leg, so someone had to carry it. Enter the good shepherd.

Sometimes, even well meaning sheep wander off. They enter into desert seasons. They enter into foolishness, or they enter into bondage. They chase after disobedience or temptation and they get their leg broken.

However, the broken sheep isn't discarded. The shepherd carried the sheep along until it was healed and did not leave it behind or alone. Because the shepherd is a good shepherd, it is likely he said to the sheep, "It's OK."

That's God. Our Good Shepherd carries us through our broken-ness, and through our foolishness. He carries us until He has seen us healed. We can trust Him.

The hope in all this is that God is carrying you. Whether you can see it or not, He is carrying you. He might have broken your leg, but if He did, it was for your survival and for your future. He loves you so much. As His sheep, we are in His arms, whether we particularly care to be or not.

He tends his flock like a shepherd: He gathers the lambs in his arms and carries them close to his heart; he gently leads those that have young. (Isaiah 40:11)

But you, O Israel, my servant, Jacob, whom I have chosen, you descendants of Abraham my friend, I took you from the ends of the earth, from its farthest corners I called you. I said, 'You are my servant'; I have chosen you and have not rejected you. So do not fear, for I am with you; do not be dismayed, for I am your God. I will strengthen you and help you; I will uphold you with my righteous right hand. All who rage against you will surely be ashamed and dis-graced; those who oppose you will be as nothing and perish. Though you search for your enemies, you will not find them. Those who wage war against you will be as nothing at all. For I am the Lord, your God, who takes hold of your right hand and says to you, Do not fear; I will help you. (Isaiah 41:8-13, NIV1984)

WHAT IT LOOKS LIKE

So, what does freedom look like?

I propose our liberty in Christ comes only when we are enslaved by our love for Christ. We cannot claim freedom in Christ until we have given ourselves over to Him, completely and totally.

We are only free to say no to evil, to lesser gods, to bondage, and to sin when we have said yes to Christ with everything that we are. The lesser chains of this world have no hold on such individuals. Desire for Christ has consumed their desire for the stuff that falls short of Christ.

We can actually choose to be desperately given over to Christ. We can choose to be a faithful Bride. We can choose to do everything in our power to add to His joy. We can choose to give Him everything, so that sin is left with nothing.

Is it hard? Yes. Is being made into a spotless Bride a lifelong process? Yes. Will we, despite our best efforts, die with a tendency to sin? Yes.

We can be so in love with Christ that even our worst stumbling fails to tether us to darkness. We can be so in love with Christ that our sin and shame do not remove us from feeling loved by the Father. In love with Jesus, we can rebuke the damages of sin. We can be so caught up in the affections of Jesus that, even in our sin, we claim the titled "beloved." We can be so enraptured by the heart of the Father that our sin and our sin nature become foreign and unfamiliar things. We can fall in love to the point that our short-fallings fail to snuff out the fact that we are fully alive. We can give ourselves to Him in such measure that our dirtiness and depravity seem silly in light of the immense love of the Father.

Remember, our righteousness is Christ, not our ability to be righteous.

That is the place of freedom. It is relationship versus religion. We will never arrive at moral perfection in this life, although we are made perfect in Christ. We will never arrive at sinlessness in this life, although Christ is our righteousness. Freedom doesn't come from the place of performance; from the place of doing or not doing. Our freedom has nothing to do with us.

Our exodus will come with the revelation of the Father's heart. It is the place of love, of knowing that we cannot stop the Father's love for us, despite our best efforts and our worst failings. It is the place of choosing to listen to the voice of faithful Jesus, rather than the lesser voices that accuse and condemn us. It's the place of rest. Liberty happens when our relationship with God hinges on the Father's love, and not on our own abilities not to sin. Life comes with the revelation that the Father sees us in Christ, and not in sin.

The Bride is free when she has been shown the perfect faithfulness of her Bridegroom, Jesus. She loses her insecurity. She loses the desire to betray her Bridegroom, who is passionately *for* her. We are free when we no longer desire to give ourselves over to the alternative, dirty lovers of creation. We are free when we have tasted and seen that God is extravagantly enough.

Father, reveal your heart to your children.

Deposit a revelation of your love in the hearts of your people.

Show us perfect love.

Amen

About the Author

Bobby Howard lives in Fayetteville, Arkansas, where he loves to drink coffee, do ministry, and call the Hogs. He graduated from the University of Arkansas with a degree in Political Science in the spring of 2013, and he works on staff at Christian Life Cathedral in Fayetteville. His current passion is to share the Father's heart with youth, young adults, and college students within the Church.

If you wish to contact the author, feel free to do so:

thefathersheartbook@gmail.com

@BobbyHoward63

CPSIA information can be obtained at www.ICGtesting.com
Printed in the USA
LVOW13s1244171113

361635LV00005B/8/P

9 781940 243146